Praise for

DYING TO

WAKE UP

"This is one of the most amazing NDEs I've ever heard, not just for the experience itself, but for the difference it has made in Dr. Parti's life."

—Dannion Brinkley, *New York Times* bestselling coauthor of *Saved by the Light*

"Dr. Parti's NDE is powerful, deeply spiritual, and transformative, not just for the man who experienced it, but for the person who reads about it, too."

—Anita Moorjani, *New York Times* bestselling author of *Dying to Be Me*

"Healed by his near-death experience, Dr. Rajiv Parti has become a healer himself—a true doctor of the soul. The story of his amazing transformation from a materialistically obsessed anesthesiologist to a spiritual teacher is one of the most inspiring I have encountered in nearly forty years of researching NDEs."

—Kenneth Ring, PhD, author of *Lessons from the Light*

"Dr. Rajiv's NDE is amazing, and the shift he made in his life afterward will melt your heart. Buy this book so that you too will wake up."

—Beverly Brodsky, coordinator, International Association of Near-Death Studies (IANDS)

"Dr. Parti's story is extraordinary, not just because his near-death experience was so profound and evidential, but because as a physician, he links science and spirit in an account that bridges both worlds."

—Terri Daniel, founder of the Death Awareness Institute and the Afterlife Conference

"A spiritual wake-up call . . . Parti's powerful story is filled with wisdom and truth that speak directly to the soul."

—Suzanne Giesemann, author of *Messages of Hope*

DYING TO

WAKE UP

*A Doctor's Voyage into the Afterlife
and the Wisdom He Brought Back*

RAJIV PARTI, MD
WITH PAUL PERRY

Foreword by Raymond A. Moody, Jr., MD, PhD

ATRIA PAPERBACK

NEW YORK   LONDON   TORONTO   SYDNEY   NEW DELHI

ATRIA
PAPERBACK

An Imprint of Simon & Schuster, Inc.
1230 Avenue of the Americas
New York, NY 10020

Copyright © 2016 by Rajiv Parti, MD, and Paul Perry

Excerpt from pages 95 to 99 from *Paranormal* by Raymond Moody, MD,
and Paul Perry. Copyright © 2012 by Raymond Moody, MD, and Paul Perry.
Reprinted by permission of HarperCollins Publishers.

First Atria Paperback edition August 2017

ATRIA PAPERBACK and colophon are trademarks of Simon & Schuster, Inc.

For information about special discounts for bulk purchases,
please contact Simon & Schuster Special Sales at 1-866-506-1949
or business@simonandschuster.com.

The Simon & Schuster Speakers Bureau can bring authors to
your live event. For more information or to book an event, contact
the Simon & Schuster Speakers Bureau at 1-866-248-3049 or
visit our website at www.simonspeakers.com.

Interior design by Kyoko Watanabe

Manufactured in the United States of America

10 9 8 7 6 5 4 3 2 1

Library of Congress Control Number: 2015037716

ISBN 978-1-4767-9731-1
ISBN 978-1-4767-9732-8 (pbk)
ISBN 978-1-4767-9733-5 (ebook)

*This book is dedicated to the Light that greets
us when we pass and to my family.*

—Rajiv Parti, MD

To Nicholas Paul Perry Mekosh, a truly grand child.

—Paul Perry

The only source of knowledge is experience.

—ALBERT EINSTEIN

If you do not change direction, you may end up where you are heading.

—LAO TZU

CONTENTS

Foreword by Raymond A. Moody, Jr., MD, PhD   xi

Introduction: The Frozen Man   1

1   The Seventh Surgery   7

2   The ER   17

3   Above It All   23

4   Tough Love from Hell   29

5   Rescued   35

6   Tunnel of Understanding   43

7   Past Life, Future Life   51

8   Future Shock   57

9   Caught by Karma   69

10   Merry Christmas   75

11   The Ladder of Enlightenment   79

CONTENTS

12 The Open Road   87

13 True Healing   93

14 Transformed by the Light   105

15 Lucky Rajiv or Poor Rajiv   117

16 The Story He Had Not Heard   123

17 Guidance   133

18 What Now?   141

19 Funeral for Myself   147

20 An Awakening   169

21 An Experiment of One   183

22 Aruba Awakening   193

23 Be Who You Are   201

24 A Shared-Death Experience   207

Conclusion: To Understand Who We Are   211

Acknowledgments   219

FOREWORD

Raymond A. Moody, Jr., MD, PhD

Two years ago I received a captivating e-mail from an anesthesiologist in Southern California. His name was Rajiv Parti, and the purpose of the e-mail was to make me aware of his profound near-death experience (NDE).

I get hundreds of e-mails and letters of this kind each year from people who simply want to tell me about their NDEs, but this one stood out for a variety of reasons, including the fact that he was a medical doctor, a profession that has as many NDEs as the regular population but generally keeps them secret for fear of being stigmatized by their peers.

But there were other reasons that this NDE was special. One was that Raj had visions of two previous lives. Although it is common to hear of past lives from those who have NDEs, Parti's experiences were different. He saw himself as an Indian prince in medieval times who was mercilessly and senselessly whipping the poor. He also saw himself two hundred years ago as an Afghani poppy farmer who was addicted to opiates from the poppies that he farmed for a living.

His past life experience was extremely detailed and presented explanations for aspects of his personality in his current life that he wanted, *needed*, to change. As he wrote in his e-mail to me, "[During my past life review] another wave of awareness washed over me: if I lived again, I would have to break these patterns completely, and live differently." Otherwise he would be destined to repeat them.

In this aspect alone, that of past lives being revealed during NDEs, the publication of Raj's otherworldly adventure will add a whole new dimension to the rational study of near-death experiences. The elements of past life memories demand attention, and the publication of his story will link the study of NDEs with reincarnation in a way that will take near-death studies in a new direction.

Another unique aspect of his NDE was a visit to hell. Accounts of such visits are rare in NDE literature. Some researchers feel they take place often, but that there is a stigma in telling of such a visit—that admitting to a hellish NDE will somehow make one evil. That wasn't the case with Raj. He fearlessly recounted his experience of hell in total, representing it as a teaching tool that revealed flaws in his character that had to be remedied. For Raj, his visit to this realm emphasized his materialistic lifestyle and gave his late father an opportunity to save his son from falling into hell, a fate worse than death. Having his father save him was especially ironic, given that the two had had a rocky relationship during his father's lifetime. Now, at the edge of hell and clearly in a spiritual world, the two bonded as they never had before, and Raj understood and forgave the harsh behavior he had been subjected to by his father. Where he was haunted by his paternal relationship, he now understood why it had gone so poorly and generously forgave his father. He also learned that the sins of the father don't have to be visited on the son, which changed the way he interacted with his own son.

As a result of these events and others covered in this book, Raj experienced a profound personality transformation. Many people who have had NDEs learn these lessons of profound transformation, and when they come back from their NDEs, they deeply change their interactions with their fellow human beings. Yet it is difficult for many to stay on this new path. They are, after all, still human beings in a human world.

Raj has stayed on track with the message of his vision, and he has done so at great cost.

After his NDE, Raj gave up his anesthesiology practice and has been working on a form of treatment called *consciousness-based healing*. This is not a form of healing he devised, but one that was revealed to him by the guardian angels that were with him during his NDE and remain with him to this day. Despite the hardships of changing the focus of his profession, Raj is dogged in his determination to bring this form of treatment into practice. His whole philosophy of healing and living has changed. As he wrote to me in that first e-mail, "My job is to put one step in front of the other and follow the path faithfully and with trust—just like I did during the NDE, holding my father's hand."

He wrote to me in that e-mail:

I was being told [by the Being of Light] that it was not my time to leave yet, and that everything would be all right but my path now was going to be as a healer. I was told that I would have to leave anesthesiology and materialism behind. The Being of Light told me: "*Now it is time to be healer of the soul, especially of the diseases of soul, of the energy body, addiction, depression, chronic pain, and cancer.*"

I was told that this was the reason I had to experience the diseases that had befallen me personally—so I could have empathy for others, so that I would know how it felt to be in their shoes.

I once had the opportunity to share the stage with Raj. It was at a small consciousness conference in Arizona where the conference organizer had asked him to tell his story. I was sitting behind him, and shortly after he began to talk, I noticed that most of the people in the audience were wiping tears from their eyes; a few were sobbing. Then I realized something I didn't expect: *tears in my own eyes.* Despite hearing tens of thousands of NDEs in my lifetime, I was deeply moved by the words of redemption that came from Raj.

In the end, he said something so profound that I had to stifle a sob:

> The future is still being formed, but in all these changes, I have felt no fear. I know I am not alone, and while I may not yet have full sight of what my future looks like, I do know that there is a plan—and that the plan is a good plan.
>
> In my old life, I used to put people to sleep. Now I wake them up. And I have woken up too.

The story contained in this book, *Dying to Wake Up*, is one of transcendence and transformation. It is one of the most astounding and complete near-death experiences I have heard in almost fifty years of investigating this phenomenon. It is powerful even to a veteran researcher like myself. It's remarkable.

DYING TO WAKE UP

Introduction

The Frozen Man

By all indications, the patient on the operating table was dead. His heart was stopped, and his body drained of blood. There was no respirator turned on to keep him breathing and no oxygen being fed to his lungs. The EKG machine that would ordinarily beep in time with his heartbeat was silent because there was nothing to beat in time with. All of his organs had stopped functioning, and his brain revealed no waves on the EEG machine.

In fact, the patient wasn't dead, not really. He was in suspended animation through a surgical procedure known as hypothermic cardiopulmonary bypass and circulatory arrest, a procedure that replaces the patient's blood with a cool fluid that lowers body temperature to approximately 50 degrees Fahrenheit and stops all bodily functions. Just like death, but not quite.

The purpose of the surgery in his case was to repair a tear in the aorta, the main artery leading from his heart. This is a dangerous surgery, but there was little choice. Without it, his weakened aorta would eventually burst and kill him instantly. If the surgery didn't kill him, he would have a normal life span. He was almost damned if he did, but definitely damned if he didn't.

I was the anesthesiologist on the case. As chief of the department of anesthesiology for the Bakersfield Heart Hospital, I was trained for these difficult and dangerous surgeries. It was my job to administer anesthesia to the patient while the surgeons opened his chest to expose the heart. Then, after the surgery, when warm blood was returned to his body, my role was to keep him safely and deeply anesthetized as we brought him back to life. In between, when the cooling solution filled the circulatory system and the patient's vital signs appeared as flat lines on the monitors, I had little to do but observe the deft hands of the surgeons as they performed their delicate and complex patchwork on this king of all arteries. They had only sixty minutes to work their magic. After that the patient would likely die or suffer neurological damage.

When we brought this patient to the operating room, he was already heavily sedated. I spoke to him momentarily when we transferred him to the operating table, but he didn't have much interest in conversation. The sedation and the realization of what was about to happen had sunk in and he remained silent, wondering, I am sure, if I was the last person he would ever see. I didn't give him much time to think about it. I injected propofol and other anesthetic drugs into the saline tube placed in an arm vein and watched him drop off to sleep. After placing an endotracheal tube into his windpipe, I watched carefully as the patient's chest was opened and his heart prepped for the surgery. Then a surgical specialist administered the cold perfusion fluid, and another carefully drained his blood into an oxygenator that would keep it primed with oxygen and clot free. Before long the patient was in suspended animation, and the surgery had begun.

Over the years I have worked on several of these operations, and they always amaze me. The genius of the research that led to this surgery, the deep concentration of the skilled surgeons—to me this procedure took medicine to a new frontier.

From my place at the head of the table, I looked down at the patient. He seemed as dead as any dead patient I have ever seen, yet he would make it back to life and be among the living for many years.

For the next hour, I watched the chief surgeon work with speed and urgency, racing against the clock to repair the damaged artery. The room was filled with controlled tension and fear, and not just because of the delicate nature of the operation. A good percentage of patients undergoing this surgery do not survive—not because of the surgery, which is almost always successful, but because the human body is not always capable of returning from the dead. *The surgery was successful but the patient died* is not considered the punch line of a joke with this operation; rather, it is a reality that we in the operating room are all too aware of.

When the surgery was completed, we moved with great efficiency to bring the patient back to life. As the blood was transfused back into his body, I administered more anesthesia so he wouldn't awaken too quickly. Then the ice was unpacked from around his head so his brain could warm up. As the cold blood was slowly warmed, platelets were added to enhance clotting, and then cardioversion paddles were activated on either side of his heart in hopes of jolting it to a start.

This was the point at which we all held our breath. If the cardioversion jolts did not restore the heartbeat, the patient would die.

On the third try, this patient's heart began to thump regularly. After several minutes observing the heartbeat, a closure surgeon stepped forward and sewed his chest together. Then this resurrected patient was taken to the intensive care unit (ICU) for recovery.

I was one of the first to greet him when he awoke. He was groggy, but he knew where he was and he was glad to be there. I think he didn't expect to be alive. When he saw me, he cracked a smile.

"I was watching you guys in the operating room," he said.

What he said clearly didn't register, and I must have looked puzzled.

"I said, I was watching you guys in the operating room," he repeated. "I was out of my body, floating around by the ceiling."

How can that be true? I asked myself. *He was frozen!*

"Yeah," he said. "I saw you just standing at the head of the table, I saw the surgeon sewing the patch on my artery, I saw that nurse . . ." And then he went on to describe the number of surgeons in the operating theater, where they were positioned, the actions of the nurses, and other events that made it clear he had been observing events from somewhere above us.

I could hardly believe what he was saying. Over the course of my twenty-five-year career, I had attended to hundreds of patients, many of whose hearts were barely beating when they arrived in the operating room. There had been patients who claimed to see deceased friends during their cardiac arrest, or who saw lights at the end of tunnels, or who claimed to see people made of light, but I chalked that off to some kind of fantasy and referred them to the psychiatrist. As one of my medical school teachers had said, "If you can't touch it, hear it, or see it on a monitor, send it to psych."

But what had happened to this man was different. He had accurately described the operating room I was working in with great clarity. He not only showed signs of being alive when his heart and brain were inert but also of being *awake*.

"Your heart was stopped," I said to him. "Your brain didn't have any activity. You couldn't have seen anything. Your head was packed in ice."

The frozen man challenged me again by describing details in the operating room he hadn't mentioned earlier—information about surgical tools and comments about things that took place well into the surgery.

He was interested in talking more, but I stopped him and ordered a shot of Haldol, a strong antipsychotic drug. The stock market had just closed, and I wanted to see how my investments had done that day. I didn't tell him that, of course. I told him a sort of truth, that I had other patients to see, and promised I would come back later to talk about his experience. I quickly made my rounds of the ICU and then hurried to my Hummer in the parking lot. Driving it made me feel like a king of the road. No car dared cross me, and if anyone did, I would tailgate them so close that I could see the fear in their eyes as they looked back at me through the rearview mirror. A half hour later, I pulled into the driveway of our Mediterranean-style mansion and ran to my home office to check the stock market on my computer.

Before long, I had forgotten about the frozen man and any indications that his consciousness had left his body.

I can't remember if the story of the frozen man made it into our family dinner conversation that night. It probably didn't. I was somewhat ashamed at not staying to listen to his story. By the next day, I decided not to visit with the frozen man. He had been moved to another department and was no longer my charge anyway. And after all, time is money. That's how materialistic I was.

Within a few days, he had become just another anecdote.

———

The day after Christmas 2010, the curious memory of the frozen man came rushing back. At the age of fifty-three, I found myself lying in the recovery room of the University of California at Los Angeles Medical Center talking to an anesthesiologist about my own near-death experience (NDE) that had just taken place during surgery.

The problem was that he didn't believe me, or else he didn't care. Like the frozen man whose NDE I had ignored myself, I now had ventured into a spiritual world and felt more alive than ever before. Not only had I completely left my body and brain behind and gone into another realm of consciousness, I had returned with an astonishing amount of wisdom that was readily available to me. I knew the other place I visited was completely real, and later it would prove itself again.

Yet as I tried to share all of this information with my colleague, I could tell he wasn't the least bit interested. In fact, when he promised to return later so I could tell him the entire story, I knew that karma, the idea that you reap what you sow, had now taken place. Just as I had promised to return to the bedside of the frozen man and listen to his story, so too was my colleague making the same promise to me. And like me, he never returned.

It has now become my life's mission, my dharma, to bring the message of consciousness-based healing to the world, to heal diseases of the soul. I deliver that message to you now in this book. A dream of spiritual peace is a common one. I want to show you how to attain it.

Chapter 1

The Seventh Surgery

It must be cold out, I thought, my teeth chattering slightly. It was December 23, 2010, hours before Christmas Eve, and it felt as if I was in the frigid Himalaya mountains of India instead of the flatlands of Bakersfield, California. I had gone upstairs to bed with an odd mix of symptoms. First I had felt very hot and tired, then cold and shaky. When I began to shiver, I reached for my iPhone and checked the outdoor temperature. It was 50 degrees Fahrenheit.

I shouldn't be shivering, I thought. As I pulled the blankets closer and felt myself get colder at the same time, I was frightened.

I could hear my wife and children downstairs, preparing for dinner. Plates were being spread out on the table, and I smelled the rich aroma of spices in the Indian food my wife was preparing. Usually such aromas would make my mouth water. Today it made me nauseous.

I covered my head and tried to blot out the television. My wife, Arpana, had turned on CNN about two hours earlier and had left me in our bedroom while she went downstairs to cook dinner. "Try to sleep," she said. "I'll wake you when dinner is ready." I took a pain pill when she left (How many had I taken that day?) and hoped it would give me the peace of sleep. It didn't. Instead it made me groggy and more angry and frightened. I could feel swelling and heat in my abdomen and scrotum, and although I had a deep need to urinate, I couldn't coax out more than a few drops.

I don't deserve this, I thought. *I'm a doctor.*

I recalled the good old days, years before the six surgeries that brought me to this point.

I had come to Bakersfield from Louisiana to work as a temporary doctor. My assignment was to work one month as an anesthesiologist in the San Joaquin Community Hospital. After years on the East Coast, it was a pleasure to be in the warmth of the San Joaquin Valley and the beauty of California. Before long, I was offered a permanent position at the hospital, and I accepted immediately.

Arpana opened a dental office of her own, and I soon changed hospitals to take a position as an anesthesiologist at the Bakersfield Heart Hospital, an institution dedicated to delicate heart surgeries. Within a few years, I was named head of anesthesiology. A few years after that I joined several of my anesthesiology colleagues in starting a pain clinic where those with chronic pain could receive treatment in an outpatient setting. Soon we were on a road to prosperity that we could hardly believe. We traded our small house for a larger one and then an *extremely* large house as we built a family of two boys, Raghav and Arjun, and a girl, Ambika.

Our cars went from average Fords and Toyotas to Mercedeses and Lexuses and then to the "supercars" like a Porsche and a Hummer. I dreamed of one day having a Ferrari in my garage that I kept wrapped in a dust cover and took out only for an occasional weekend spin. My goal was bigger *everything*—house, cars, art collection, bank accounts. At one point in my twenty-five years at the heart hospital, I took a nine-month sabbatical in order to trade stock. I made millions of dollars, sometimes a million dollars in one day, but I lost it as fast as I made it because I thought I could read the direction of the stock market with greater accuracy than the pros. That didn't happen, and I finally gave up this folly and returned to the hospital.

The goal of my neighbors in the mini-castles around me was the same. Every new house built on the block usually had more square footage than the others. It would have been funny had it not been so serious. Size matters, especially when one is building a monument to oneself for the scale of immortality.

The houses in this neighborhood were all designed to match the image the owner wanted to project. There were Mediterranean villas (ours), Spanish casitas, ultramoderns, and even one home that was a mini-replica of the White House. It was a monstrosity to look at, but everyone in the neighborhood understood the motivation behind it. How else could the owners show they were as big and important as the president of the United States? (The owner sold cars for a living.)

Driving through the neighborhood was like a spin through Disneyland. But driving through the neighborhood would have been totally impossible for those without the pass code for several gates. The community was hermetically sealed, safe from the outside world, and I had come to believe that meant safe from physical illness as well. *Doctors don't get sick.* I had come to believe that. *And if we do, we can treat the illness immediately, stop it in its tracks.*

That is how I viewed myself: a master of my fate, a miracle worker who was immune to all ailments.

Feeling like a master of the universe is easy in the world of modern medicine. In my specialty alone, heart surgery anesthesia, the medical world had made so many advances in technology and techniques that we could literally bring patients back from the dead by doing everything from unclogging an artery with a balloon to replacing it or even dropping in a transplanted heart. The cardio-vascular death rate has declined 40 percent in the last decade due to advances like those we administered on a routine basis in our heart hospital. Families wept for joy at the end of a successful heart procedure because they knew we had added many years, perhaps decades, to the life of a loved one.

Maybe it's a sense of cheating death for others that gives cardiac surgical teams the vague feeling that we can overcome our own death. Of course that isn't true. The goal can't be to live forever because no one does, at least not in this body. The goal should be to create a *legacy* that will live forever. To think of life in any other way is just a myth, the one I was living.

Reality popped that myth for me. In 2008 a routine physical revealed a significant increase in my PSA count, an indication that I had prostate cancer. A biopsy of the prostate gland told me how bad it was. "I have good news and bad news for you," said my urologist and good friend who called one evening while my wife and I sat drinking tea in the backyard by the golf course our house overlooked. "You have prostate cancer. But it's in its early stages, and you can have it taken out and you'll be cured."

I was fifty-one and in shock. And angry. *Why me? What did I do to deserve this?*

We went to one of the best prostate surgeons in the country, located across the country in Miami, Florida. I told him I was worried about incontinence, about impotency. He told me not to worry: "I can almost guarantee no complications. After a few weeks you will be back to normal." He was a genius of this walnut-sized gland and a colleague as well. Why should I doubt what he said?

We scheduled surgery using a procedure known as laparoscopic radical prostatectomy, removal of the entire prostate through small holes in the abdomen using tube-shaped instruments fitted with a video camera and cutting instruments. Within days of the surgery, it was clear that I was going to be incontinent and impotent. The surgeon was sorry. I was angry.

Scar tissue closed my urethra not once but three times. And each time surgeons in Bakersfield had to operate, using laser beams to vaporize the scar tissue. The postsurgical pain was so intense I was forced to take pain pills. I took a lot, and when the pain abated, I continued to take the pills, looking forward to the pleasurable buzz they gave me, along with their painkilling effects.

A fifth surgery at UCLA Medical Center took care of the scarring problem with the direct injection of an antiscarring drug, but by now the incontinence had become intolerable. I had to wear an adult diaper, changing it every two or three hours to avoid getting diaper rash. This was almost impossible, since many of the heart surgeries were long and involved, taking five to six hours sometimes. When that happened, I ran the risk of infection, which required stronger and stronger antibiotics and more pain pills.

Finally my UCLA surgeon recommended an artificial sphincter, an implanted mechanical device that would allow me to control my bladder with the touch of a button strategically placed under the skin. I had the sixth surgery done on December 13, 2010.

But now, less than two weeks later, something horrible had gone wrong: an infection around the artificial sphincter had spread and was filling my abdomen with pus.

I started taking the most powerful antibiotics available at the beginning of the infection. I began with a heavy dose of oral Keflex, and when that didn't work, I was switched to Cipro, a heavy hitter in the treatment of urinary tract infections. That didn't work either. Now, the night before Christmas Eve, I could feel the heat and pressure build around my pelvic area, symptoms of a rapidly rising infection.

Arpana came into the room from the kitchen downstairs. She held a tasty hors d'oeuvre plate of mixed treats for me to sample, but when she looked at me, her expression turned to alarm. She nearly dropped the plate as she set it down and pulled back the blanket to look at my face.

"Oh my God," she said, picking up a thermometer. She shook it and slipped it under my tongue. In a few moments, the mercury rose to 105 degrees.

She rushed downstairs and called UCLA Medical Center, where surgeons had implanted the artificial sphincter. I later learned that when they connected her to the surgeon and she said I had a 105-degree temperature, he told her to get me to the hospital as quickly as possible.

I could hear little of this phone conversation from upstairs. But what I could hear were desperate whispers and hurried conversations and then the rush of the entire family running up the stairs.

Arpana sat me on the edge of the bed and helped me dress, while our children gathered in the room. They watched with fear as their weeping mother struggled to dress me.

"Help us!" she said to our three children. Cautiously they helped me stand and braced me as they took me downstairs, one uncertain step at a time. In the few minutes it took to make it into the front seat of my wife's BMW, I was exhausted. A fever of such magnitude leaves one both burning hot and shivering cold, a contradicion of symptoms. My daughter covered me with a blanket, and Arpana started the car, tears streaming down her face. She was frightened by my condition and told me later that she was afraid I might worsen quickly in transit. And then in the middle of the mountains that were between home and the hospital, what would she do?

I tried to get comfortable in the car and ignore my wife's sobs as she accelerated onto the freeway and headed south to Los Angeles, one hundred miles away. I was beginning to wish she had called an ambulance.

The fever and infection had my thoughts in a swirl. As we sped toward Los Angeles, all I could think about were the negatives in my life, a long list that could be organized as: Unlucky, Cancer Patient, Infection Prone, Addict, Depressive, Materialistic, Demanding, Unloving, Egotist, Angry.

Denial of my own illness made me angry with myself. *I'm a doctor. Why didn't I know something was terribly wrong?* The truth was that I did know something was terribly wrong. I just didn't act. Like most other doctors, I didn't take kindly to illness in my own body and was now paying for my denial.

My anger spread to other events in my life. First, I became angry with God for giving me prostate cancer. *What possible good is it to give me such a horrible disease? Why did I deserve something like this?*

And then there were the pain pills. As my wife drove me to the hospital that night, I finally admitted to myself that I had crossed the threshold of addiction. The medical definition of *addiction* is to take more than is prescribed. Because of the surgeries and their complications, I had been prescribed pain pills for my pelvic pain. At first they worked for me, helping me get through the aftermath of the surgeries and the subsequent infections. But as the pain continued, the effect of the narcotics lessened, making routine work and home life more difficult. I took more and stronger doses, longing to stay in control. I finally learned what some of my patients already knew: how easy it is to qualify as an addict when all you long for is to be pain free.

And there was more. The combination of the cancer and my pill addiction had depressed me. To cope with that condition, I had started taking antidepressants. Soon I felt as if they were as necessary to my well-being as the pain pills. Based on my medical training and through addiction specialists at the hospital, I knew that I would have to go to an inpatient facility for at least twelve weeks to end my pill addiction. *Why had I lost control of my life?*

My son Raghav came to mind. Because he was my eldest, I had been much harder on him than on my other children, expecting him to follow in my footsteps. But he had been in medical school for three years now and was not doing well. Although he had been willing to attend medical school, he lacked enthusiasm, and his grades reflected his disinterest in becoming a physician. Still I had stubbornly insisted that he continue his studies.

Over the years, I had adopted my father's and grandfather's Indian theory of child raising, which could be summed up in one often repeated phrase: "A bent nail must be straightened with a hammer." And though my father never used a hammer, he "straightened me," as his father had straightened him, whenever he thought I was not living up to my intellectual potential. Though physical punishment was typical in India at the time, I swore I would never lay a hand on my children. But over the years, my father's anger became my anger, and I had frequently punished my children with it.

Now Raghav probably feared me, perhaps even hated me. *Would I have a chance to make it up to him?* I wondered as the car roared through this endless night. *Where is my son now? Why isn't he in this car with me now that I really need him?*

By the time we pulled into the emergency medical entrance at UCLA, my anger had spread like fire to every part of my life until it touched the truth. *My life is my responsibility. I should have been more careful in choosing my path.*

When I reached that conclusion, I must have audibly gasped, because one of the attendants who loaded me on the stretcher gave my hand a squeeze of assurance.

"You're safe at the hospital now," he said.

I don't know if I shook my head or nodded. I did know the frightening facts in front of me: that I had a 105-degree temperature and a pelvic infection that antibiotics couldn't touch.

Based on the speed of this infection, I wasn't sure I would have another chance. In fact, I supposed I was going to die.

Chapter 2

The ER

There was no lack of medical personnel in the UCLA Emergency Room. Despite being the Christmas season, doctors, nurses, and medical assistants swarmed around me. A nurse took my wrist and checked my pulse, another took my temperature, an ER doctor listened to my heart with a stethoscope, another doctor shined a light in my eyes. There were so many doctors and nurses around my gurney that Arpana was pushed into the background, her concerned face growing smaller behind a wall of blue scrubs.

I appreciated the medical attention but also knew what it meant. My surgeon had called the ER and made his concerns known about a surgical patient with a high temperature. It's exactly what I would have done in his position. A postsurgical temperature of this magnitude meant that infection could seep into my bloodstream, where it would rapidly spread throughout my entire body. This septic shock carries a death rate of higher than 60 percent, and once it begins, it can be difficult to stop.

"We need to catheterize him," said one of the doctors, pressing on my engorged bladder hard enough to make me moan. "He doesn't appear to be able to urinate, and I don't want his kidneys to shut down."

"Amen," said another voice.

Amen . . . Amen . . . I repeated to myself. I had begun to shiver hours ago, and now I was trembling uncontrollably. It was a strange feeling. I could feel the heat of the temperature and the chill of my muscles and organs as they struggled to cope with the infection that was overwhelming their metabolism. *I'm too hot to be cold and too cold to be hot,* I thought. *I am dying.*

A nurse inserted an IV into my arm and connected it to a bottle of saline solution to keep me hydrated. Then she injected it with a prescribed dose of narcotics to relax me for the painful procedure that was about to come.

I heard the screech of the privacy curtain being pulled around my bed. In a fog of pain and fever, I could make out one of the nurses as she fumbled with a prelubricated catheter tube. The narcotics had relaxed me, but not so much that I didn't feel pain as the tube was inserted into my urethra. The pain was followed by great relief as my bladder drained completely. I unwound as pressure left my body, and I sank deeper into the gurney.

"Thank you," I mumbled.

Then I fell asleep.

Two hours passed. I was very groggy. By examining the medical records later, I know only that I was given antibiotics intravenously and an ultrasound was done on my abdomen while I was asleep. Looking back, it was as if I was dead to the world, which strikes me as ironic given what occurred later when I was given the more powerful narcotic drugs of anesthesia.

What I do remember is eventually coming out of a fog to a cadre of nurses gathered around my gurney and preparing me for surgery. My abdomen was being shaved, lines inserted in my veins, bags of saline solution dangling on stainless-steel poles. I tried to take charge.

"Where's the surgeon? I need to know what's happening," I said.

A surgeon in scrubs appeared. He had a surgical mask on his face and held his hands like a praying mantis, a sign that his hands were scrubbed for surgery and ready to be gloved. He cut to the chase as only a surgeon can.

"Your ultrasound shows us that you're full of infection," he said. "You have a severe infection that we can't touch with antibiotics when you are full of pus. We need to clean it out to make you well."

He was very loud, and I had the impression that he had already told me the purpose of my upcoming surgery at least once. When he felt relatively certain that I had understood the gravity of the situation, he turned to his other duties and left me alone with my thoughts.

Severe infection . . . clean out the infection. It was a surgery I had expected but was frightening nonetheless. I feared the possibility of sepsis, an overwhelming immune response to infection. Sometimes such infection can come from a pinprick and at other times a more traumatic event. Patients whose appendix rupture often have sepsis. In that case, the appendix breaks and the contents of the intestines spill into the body cavity, infecting it with pathogens that overwhelm the immune system's ability to fight them off. My case was in between a pinprick and a ruptured appendix. The infection in my surgical site had spread and become so bad that it filled my pelvis with pus.

I had been involved in one case like my own. I was on a surgical team in San Joaquin Hospital in California that spent several hours swabbing the infection from a man whose appendix had burst. Afterward one of my colleagues said it was like cleaning up a sewage spill with a mop. We had a good laugh over that image, but it did not seem funny to me now, not when I was the patient.

I slipped back into a fog, remembering the messy details of the surgery I was about to have.

I awoke in the operating room.

Everyone's back was turned to me, each filling out charts or lining up surgical instruments, all of them getting ready for the business of my surgery. It was almost as though I wasn't there. I remembered how a patient reacted to this very scene during one of my own cases. He had raised his head from the table and said, "Hey, you guys, I'm over here!"

My eyes roamed the room and settled on the anesthesiologist, the role I would have occupied had I been working this case. He was focused on his equipment and his paperwork to make certain I got the right dose of anesthesia. I looked at him for what seemed like an eternity before he looked back.

"I'm an anesthesiologist too," I said.

"I noticed that," he said.

"What are you giving me?" I asked.

"The usual," he replied.

I knew that meant propofol, the anesthesia of choice because it puts a patient to sleep through surgery. It is a short-acting hypnotic that is jokingly referred to as "milk of amnesia" because of its milky color as an IV preparation but also because it creates a state in which the patient cannot remember anything that happens during surgery. Since propofol is not a painkiller, fentanyl was also being added to the mix. Fentanyl is a powerful pain reliever aimed at stopping the agonizing pain that could certainly accompany this messy surgery.

This combination of anesthesia drugs was the only positive thing I could think of as I lay on the operating table. These two drugs combined lead to a state of unconsciousness, like a sleep of death, because the patient knows nothing, remembers nothing, feels nothing. That was exactly how I wanted it. This was now my seventh surgery for this prostate problem. In between those surgeries were periods of pain and suffering as the scarring came back, and with it the variety of humiliations that can take place in such a delicate area. It was ironic to me that only one of the surgeries dealt with the cancer itself, the removal of the prostate gland, and four of the rest for scarring in the urethra.

None of this seems fair, I thought as the surgical nurses moved a tray of gleaming surgical instruments into place. I was covered with a thin sheet and could feel the air-conditioning delivering a crisp coolness to the operating room. I shivered, but it had nothing to do with the cold. It was the kind one gets when facing the unknown. I had seen it many times with patients facing heart surgery as I sat at the top of the operating table ready to deliver anesthesia. Sometimes they would weep and ask if they really needed to have the surgery. Others would ask about their chances of surviving the surgery. One elderly man cried for his mother who was long dead. Others would pray, and not always silently.

On this day I did none of the above. I stayed as cool and stoic as I could, believing what my medical school professors had said in class: "A doctor must always be the calmest person in the room. If they lose their nerve, everyone panics."

Is that true if they are patients? I wondered. *Is it true when we are in emergency surgery and on the other end of the knife?*

"Are you ready?" asked the surgeon, suddenly appearing above me. He waved his gloved hand at the anesthesiologist, and I was asleep before I could answer.

Chapter 3

Above It All

Is it over? Is the surgery over?

I was zooming straight up as if in an elevator, I was sure of it. It was that feeling in the pit of the stomach when you are rocketing to the fiftieth floor in a skyscraper, and the mild G-forces tug steadily at your insides. *Or is that really what I felt?* My consciousness began to lift, and instead of seeing the doctor standing over me, I could see the ceiling approaching, its glossy surface getting slowly closer.

There was a horrible smell in the room, and when I rolled over and looked down, I could see that it was emanating from my abdomen, where one of the surgeons had made several incisions and was now sucking out the infection with a bulb syringe. The odor of the pus was overwhelming and repellent. As the surgeon and a nurse diligently sucked tubes of pus into the bulb syringe and squirted them into a stainless-steel bowl, another nurse applied eucalyptus oil over their masks to take the edge off the infection's odor.

They seemed to have forgotten to dab the scented oil on the anesthesiologist's mask because he appeared to be having a problem with the powerful stench. Apparently, the odoriferous conditions reminded him of an off-color joke, which he told as he struggled with the odor.

I won't repeat the joke, but everyone in the operating theater laughed, including me. From my position above, I could see the hard work presented by my case and knew as an anesthesiologist that one of the roles of my specialty was to provide humor during difficult surgery. I made it a point to remember the joke for use in my own repertoire, which came in handy later in proving the case for my out-of-body presence in the operating room.

I was mesmerized by the scene below me. I had attended hundreds of surgeries as an anesthesiologist, but never my own and never from such a unique perspective. For a few moments, I was frightened that whatever was holding me up would suddenly stop doing so and I would slam down on my own body like a doppelgänger in free fall. But then I relaxed and watched in rapt amazement as the surgeons and nurses irrigated the infection from the recesses around my organs with purified water and swabbed it out with gauze held at the end of forceps.

While the "cleanup team" worked diligently to remove the smelly pus from my body cavity, another surgeon had made an incision lower down and was now struggling to dismantle the artificial sphincter that was the cause of the infection. The removal of the device, they hoped, would prevent further infection and allow me to live a normal life.

And a normal life was what I was feeling now. It had been several minutes since I had separated from my body, and in retrospect I can say that I was enjoying the new perspective. Below, I could see my face in a state of total repose as though nothing was going on with the body it represented. *Is that really me, or is this really me?* I wondered. There was an endotracheal tube inserted in my mouth to keep my airway open, and as best as I could tell, the only signs of life were the rhythmic moving of my chest as I breathed and the numbers and lines on the monitor that revealed my heart rate and blood pressure. I felt a pressure in my chest and became alarmed. It felt as though my heart was skipping beats. I wanted to tell them how I would handle this emergency, but I was not able to communicate with them. *How can I be in both places at once? Can I really be down there and up here at the same time, conscious while my body is unconscious?*

I struggled with this question but only briefly, because it was no longer a question but an actuality: there is a soul, and it can survive outside the body.

I had no idea what to do with this information. It flashed in my mind that I would eventually have to talk about it to my colleagues, all of whom were taught, as I was, that if there was a soul, it did not make its presence known. That attitude seemed to appease everyone in medical school, spiritual and nonspiritual alike, because it clearly established the policy of medical education toward spiritual matters. "Seeing is believing, and you can't see the spiritual," one of my professors had said.

Clearly there was now an ironic truth in what the professor said. *Seeing is believing,* and I was now in my spirit body seeing my physical body. Telling my colleagues what I was now experiencing would be a karmic experience. I had ignored patients who told me they had left their body during surgery. Would the members of my own profession now ignore me? Or, worse, would they mock me behind my back?

I began to focus on the surgeon who was removing the sphincter. He had both his hands inside my lower abdomen, twisting the mechanical device to take it apart and clean it of any infection-causing agent. I watched carefully as his deft hands filled my abdomen, twisting back and forth. *Why can't I feel what he's doing?* I asked myself. *This should be extremely painful, but I feel nothing even though it is happening to me.*

Suddenly something happened. As a man of science, the first thing that occurred to me was that someone had added an LSD-like drug called ketamine to the anesthesia. But why would the anesthesiologist do that? Even as I asked the question, I knew he would not. Something simply happened that I did not yet understand. All I know was that an extraordinary shift had taken place in my perspective. It was as though my field of vision became much wider and my consciousness expanded well beyond whatever it had been before, as though all of my senses had the ability to see, and what they saw could easily be different scenes.

At first I tried to ignore this shift in perspective. It was frightening to have so much input, and some of the visions that appeared on the edge of my sight—I would call it *mind sight*—were unpleasant.

My mind sight gravitated to the most pleasant of the images, a vivid and simple vision of my mother and sister sitting on a sofa in the lounge of our family home seven thousand miles away in New Delhi. They were relaxed and talking, with that unspoken love between mother and daughter so clear. The scene was vivid and detailed. My sister was wearing blue jeans and a red sweater and my mother a green sari and a green sweater.

My spirit body moved into the lounge with them, and my spirit ears listened to what they had to say. *Mom,* I said. She did not hear me. *Mom!* I said, reaching for her and then through her. *Mom, I'm here!* My hands passed through her as if she was made of clouds. *Or am I the one made of clouds?* I wondered.

"What should we make for dinner?" my sister asked.

"It's cold outside," Mom said. "We should make hot soup. Lentil sounds good."

Their conversation continued. They talked about the horrible pollution in New Delhi and laughed about a family friend who had recently purchased an expensive and fast BMW, only to realize that the city roads were so congested with cars, scooters, and people that he could drive no faster than those who slogged along the road next to him.

As they went into the kitchen to make dinner, my sister spoke proudly of her successful window-covering company. I stood close to them and tried to communicate, to no avail. Even though I had always been close to my mother, she could not sense my spirit body.

Still, I was mesmerized by what I saw and heard, and so focused on my mother and sister that the sudden sound of instruments clanking in the operating room frightened me. I turned my head to the left, the direction from which the sounds were coming, and I could see into the operating theater. I couldn't understand the perspective, and it frightened me. To the right were my mother and sister in New Delhi and to the left, my body on a surgical table in Los Angeles. Seven thousand miles separated the two scenes, yet both were there in front of me.

"Put more of that oil on my mask," I heard the surgeon say, turning his head toward a nurse who dabbed more eucalyptus oil under his nose. "This guy is a mess. He's lucky to be here. Give me more swabs."

I was now frightened. *What is going on?* The laws of physics were violated by what was happening. I was out of my body and floating, an untethered consciousness. But now I was able to be in at least three places at once. I have since heard of out-of-body experiences being called "bilocation" because the spiritual body is observing the physical body. But what was happening to me was "trilocation." I could see my anesthetized body, my distant family, and both from my hovering soul.

I was a mechanistic medical doctor, and this event represented new physical laws that I didn't understand. *How can I be hovering? Where is my brain, and what am I seeing with? Am I breathing? Why can I hear? Will I ever get back into my body, or am I destined to roam through eternity, a spirit without a body? Will I see others out there like me?*

I had no answers for any of these questions, just more questions. I thought about the last few years since my cancer diagnosis and how my life had gone from bad to worse. Now things were going from strange to stranger. I didn't know what to make of it. *Am I dead? Is this what death is like?*

I felt like an astronaut who had left his spacesuit, only to find that a suit was unnecessary to begin with.

I looked at my body and the surgeons in action and then at my mother and sister talking so quietly on the sofa. I looked back and forth at these scenes until they faded like a fast-setting sun.

Then I felt overwhelmed with fear. *Something's happening!* I could feel it.

Chapter 4

Tough Love from Hell

I would have been glad to stay with my mother until surgery ended, but the universe had other plans.

My world turned dark, and for a moment I was relieved. *I'm returning to my body,* I thought. But that relief was replaced by fear as I saw a distant lightning storm off to my right, one that seemed to draw me in very quickly and soon became loud with the sound of thunder and ... *What is that?* ... screams and moans of pain and anguish as wildfire moved over burned souls that withered from the intense heat. I was made to lie on a bed of nails, where their needle sharpness tortured my flesh.

I was drawn in as if on a moving sidewalk that took me to the edge of this flaming canyon. Smoke filled my nostrils and with it the sickening odor of burning flesh. I was on the lip of hell.

I tried to turn away and couldn't. I tried to move back but couldn't. Every time I took a step back, an unseen force moved me forward, leaving me with a horrific view of the most agonizing place one could ever imagine.

Naraka, I thought, the Hindu word for hell. Although I hadn't lived in India for decades, it was the Hindi word that imprinted itself in my mind as I tried fruitlessly to move away from the conflagration before me. Another name came to mind, Yama, the Hindu god of death. *He will be arriving soon*, I thought. *And then my soul will be burned with those other burning souls.*

What is my karma? A million thoughts rushed through my head as I wondered why I was there. *What is my karma?*

In my religion, karma means that your future life will be determined by your behavior in this life and previous lives.

You have clearly not been making love, I heard.

I heard this message as though it were spoken in my ear. *You have clearly not been making love.* I looked around and could see no one at my sides. The message came to me telepathically, but it was so powerful that it may well have been spoken by God.

"You have led a materialistic and selfish life," the voice said.

I knew what I heard was true, and I felt ashamed.

Over the years, I had lost empathy for my patients. I did my work like a machine, not a human being. I saw my patients as profit centers, people who could give me the wealth and prestige I wanted in exchange for my services as an anesthesiologist. I was a doctor who did his job well but cared very little that he was working on a human being.

If I showed interest in a patient as a human being, it was because that person could somehow enrich me with his or her status or contribute to my personal wealth. Patients who were less wealthy or smart found me to be a dismissive doctor whose goal was to treat them quickly and efficiently.

Standing on the rim of hell, I remembered a woman who had

come to my pain clinic for treatment of chronic arthritis. She was in substantial physical pain, but that was not why she was weeping.

"I need to talk to you, Doctor," she said. "My husband is dying of lung cancer, and I don't know what to do."

"I would love to talk to you," I said, writing out a prescription for pain and sleeping pills and handing it to her. "But I have several patients waiting." And I left.

I remembered another tragedy I had coldly ignored. We couldn't restart a patient's heart on which we had just done open heart surgery. We "zapped" his heart several times with a defibrillator, but it still wouldn't start. The distraught surgeon kept trying. Many, many times he zapped the heart, waited, and then zapped again. Finally he declared the patient dead.

We left the operating room and walked slowly down the hall to tell the family that their patriarch was dead. The surgeon was deeply moved. His voice cracking with emotion, his shoulders slumped as he told them the bad news. The distraught family hugged and wept as they realized they would never talk to their loved one again.

I felt nothing as this brief conversation transpired. All I thought about was my next case and getting home to my computer so I could play the stock market. I was like a robot. I had trained myself to blunt my emotions. And then, even something a robot doesn't do, I had trained myself to think only of myself. To some extent this was a necessary response. Within a half hour, there would be another patient to cheer up and prepare for surgery. It was a stressful life, and I didn't take time to process my emotions. Instead I drank two or three glasses of scotch in the evening and was up at 6:00 a.m. I would drive to the hospital while I drank coffee and ate a sandwich in the car. Before going into surgery, I would check the stock market to make sure my most precious asset was on track. I had clearly hidden my emotions behind a wall of possessions.

As the smoke billowed and the burning souls screamed around me, I thought of my possessions and how meaningless they were. *Why do I have these things?* I had a home so big that when we were in different parts of the house we had to communicate using our iPhones. I was in constant competition with my neighbors and colleagues, and as a result I had accumulated things. There was no end to my avarice. My life had become a runaway American dream.

My desire for wealth had caused a lot of stress in my life even before my prostate cancer diagnosis. Like many other professionals, I relieved my stress with alcohol, drinking on the nights I was not on call and on my free weekends. However it might have affected my long-term health, I soon discovered that for the short term, I persuaded myself that a good night's sleep was all I needed to be in complete charge of my faculties.

Five years earlier, I had torn a ligament in my right wrist. It was extremely painful, and I sometimes mixed pain pills and alcohol. The combination was dangerous, and I knew it. I'd even warned patients about it. Still, I convinced myself that I could drink and take pain pills safely as long as I didn't exceed my prescription dosage and indulged in them when there was sufficient time to recover from the highs that made me think I knew all and could see all. As my wrist pain lessened, I stopped taking the pain pills, confident that I was still in control. Only later did I realize this was common thinking among addicts. At the time, though, I didn't believe I could be an addict. I knew too much about the human condition. I was, after all, a highly qualified physician.

This warped view of my existence reminded me of another harsh fact about my life that seemed benign until now: I was always protected by walls. To get to or from my neighborhood, I had to pass through two electronic gates, one with a guard. When I drove to work, I was hermetically sealed in the comfort of a luxury car. When I was at the hospital, I was in an operating room or my office. At home I spent most of my time watching TV and very little time talking with my wife and children. Since the pain meds made me moody, I doubt that my children wanted much to do with me anyway. I lived inside my own carefully constructed bubble. I had forgotten about illness and death. I had forgotten about fate and destiny.

But fate and destiny had not forgotten me. In 2008 I began to feel a nagging discomfort in my prostate and went to see a urologist for a biopsy. A week or so later, on a pleasant fall afternoon, my wife and I sat in the backyard having high tea and admiring the carpet of green that was the golf course outside our backyard wall. Tea was a ritual we had carried with us from India, a daily habit that made it seem as though nothing in our lives would ever change.

But when Dr. Chen called, interrupting our afternoon, I knew change was coming. He nervously delivered what he said was "good *and* bad news." The good news was that the cancer he found during my prostate biopsy was contained within the prostate and had not spread to other parts of my body. The bad news was that I had to have my prostate removed.

That was when the walls surrounding me crumbled and a chain reaction of illness, depression, pill addiction, and multiple surgeries placed me here, gazing out over hell.

No wall can protect me from my karma. I have treated my fellow man poorly. Now I must suffer for the way I have treated others. I have become the victim of my own fate.

My thoughts turned to my family and how I was sometimes verbally abusive. This was particularly true of the way I treated our son Raghav. Of our three children, Raghav was the one for whom

I had the greatest expectations. As the eldest, he was expected to achieve the most in life, and I pushed him hard to do just that.

I never bothered until much later to ask him what he wanted to do with his life. Instead I made it clear that it was what *I* wanted to do with *his* life that was important.

"You are not working hard enough," I shouted angrily when his grades reflected a lack of understanding of the subject I loved.

Though my words were not as cruel as those of my father, my voice and manner were just as wrathful and furious. I was being as thoughtlessly mean to my own son as my father had been to me. I had become a reflection of my father.

On these occasions, I was ashamed, but I pretended my ire was righteous. I would tell my shocked family that Raghav deserved to be punished, and I would leave the room in a huff. I pretended to be indignant, but I was as shocked as they were by my own actions. I felt I should return and apologize, and ask for my wife and children's forgiveness, but my ego wouldn't let that happen. And so I created a worse wound in all of us by ignoring my behavior.

Now, on the rim of hell, I felt my chance to heal the past was gone. I was drained of energy, frightened and ashamed. I feared the future and that I was going to be pulled into the pit of fire and burn for eternity. Yet at the same time I was steeped in shame at the self-centered life I had lived and the lack of empathy I had expressed for my fellow humans.

There appeared to be no way out, but I prayed for one anyway. *My God, give me another chance. Please give me another chance.*

Chapter 5

Rescued

From the corner of my eye I could see my second chance coming. It came from the last person I ever expected to see. It was my father!

I recognized him immediately although he looked at least thirty years younger than when he died. His hair was jet black and he looked sleek and handsome in his official uniform as a Director of Civil Aviation. Between witnessing hell and meeting my father, I was now badly shaken. My shock must have been apparent because my father took my hand in his and led me away from the edge of hell like I was a little boy.

Putting his arm around me, he tried to comfort me. That act of empathy was frightening. I realized that I couldn't remember one occasion when my father had ever comforted me as a child. Like many Indian fathers of that generation and the generation before, the only time he or my grandfather touched me was to commit an act of punishment. That is what I expected now.

Imagine that, I thought. *At the age of fifty-three I am still afraid that my father is going to beat me.* That I could expect such a violent interaction at this late age is an indication of the dysfunction in our relationship. For the first time in decades, as my father led me from the rim of hell, I glimpsed our dysfunction in a new way. Was it possible that my father's harshness had been motivated by fear?

But I had no time to contemplate an answer to this surprising question. Instead, as he held my hand, I was overwhelmed by vivid childhood memories, the ones that made me fear this man so much that his threat of discipline or even a critical look could sometimes make me lose my dinner. Even though he was now smiling at me with great fondness, my hands felt wet with nervous perspiration and I had difficulty meeting his gaze. I had become a teenage boy again who expected a slap or an angry rebuke. No matter how insignificant my disobedience in those days, I was confident I ran the risk of physical rebuke from any object my father deemed a weapon of discipline. At the very least, I was sure to be labelled an "idiot," "fool," or "worthless."

Instead of taking pleasure in this afterlife reunion, I found myself embedded in my early life, reliving an event that took place in high school.

I was in the tenth grade and for the third straight day I had foolishly decided to ditch school with some of the bad boys. Our goal was typical of truancy in those days. As we had done for the past two days, we planned to go to several movies at a downtown theater and smoke as many cigarettes as we could. When the headmaster called my father at home and asked where I had been the last three days, my father became furious. As usual, my mother tried to calm him but he resisted her pleas for forgiveness. "That boy doesn't understand what he's doing," he sternly told my mother. "You always take his side, but if a nail is bent you must hammer it to make it straight!"

I knew what that phrase meant and what was coming. My principal had once beat me with a cane and corporal punishment was an acceptable form of punishment at home and school.

As I expected, my father confronted me in my bedroom and demanded to know where I had been the last three days. When I told him, he grabbed my cricket bat and beat me on the buttocks and the back of my legs. All the while he swore at me, his anger burning me like flaming cinders.

I know now that there were many fathers around the world who would have done the same to their sons, but even if I had known that, it would not have lessened my fear and distrust of my father. I am sure that any son who is beaten as I was must suffer the same fear and distrust. I was so bruised from the beating, I could not return to school for several days.

Standing with my father in the afterlife, I had a flashback of that event in which I relived not only how I felt being beaten but how my father felt as well. I could intuit his anger and disappointment like it was my own. It was a confusing and painful perspective because I could see everything that happened to me on that long ago day yet, at the same time, experience all that he felt and saw in those superheated moments.

What I discovered in my father's mind wasn't hatred, but fear. He was frightened that I would not take advantage of my intellectual talents and might instead choose "the left path," a phrase in Indian culture that means the wrong road.

And for the first time, I understood the source of his apprehension. In his life he had not taken the left path, nor had he taken the right one. Instead, a series of historical events forced him to create his own path.

When Pakistan became a Muslim nation in 1947, Hindus like my father, who lived in the newly-formed country, were forced to migrate across the new border to India. This migration was not peaceful. The Muslims wanted to "purify" their own country and did so by killing thousands of Hindus.

At age eighteen, my father wanted to flee from Pakistan as quickly as possible. To avoid the roads, he hopped a train to the border and travelled for miles on a flatbed car with hundreds of other terrified Hindus. Somewhere near the border, gunmen attacked the train, mercilessly peppering the helpless Hindu passengers with bullets. Dozens of people died. The lucky ones like my father hid motionless under the dead bodies until the train reached the border.

But the hatred didn't stop once he was in India.

Angry Hindus on the other side of the border accused my father of being Muslim and refused to give him water or to feed him. Out of desperation, he pulled his pants down to show the mob that he was uncircumcised. Since Islam mandates that Muslims be circumcised, the Hindus knew he was a brother. They gladly fed him a simple meal that he ate with gratitude, turning his back on the flatbed train cars loaded with the unlucky dead.

From that point on, he pulled his pants down many times to quell vengeful gunmen or to convince those with spare food that he was a worthy Hindu. By the time he got to New Delhi, my father had been humiliated dozens of times, all because one religion couldn't get along with another.

I had heard this story before, but I had never appreciated how violence and terror must have shaped my father's character. Now I did. Finally, I knew my father's need for dignity and respect and realized why he loved to wear his work uniform even on his days off. His dream to have a university education and become a medical doctor had been swept away by mob violence, religious animosity, hunger, death, and abuse.

Until this moment, my childhood fear of my father had prevented me from recognizing the fears that drove him. Walking from the rim of hell with his arm around me, I finally understood the source of what I'd once regarded as my father's despotism and felt compassion for his suffering. He was lucky to be alive and to have a job.

But he didn't feel lucky. He felt like a victim.

I recalled a phrase he had repeated often. "You work hard now for a few years or you work hard all your life. You choose." But he had chosen for me, perhaps even on the day I was born. I could see how his longing for control over his life evolved into what I saw as physical and verbal tyranny over mine. Though I now realize that his tyranny was born of love, I still resisted his conviction that I had to fear him—that only fear would put me on the right path and protect me from what he had endured.

But even a thin pancake has two sides. Embraced by my father in the afterlife, he silently reminded me that he had never beaten me again, that he had changed and how those changes made us both better people.

At my mother's insistence, we began a new routine after that last beating. He woke me every day at 4 a.m. and tutored me in reading and math. He even stayed with me in those early morning hours to keep me from falling back to sleep. My dread of facing another beating like the first one kept my nose in my books and soon I actually looked forward to my pre-dawn study sessions. This time my fears forged a love of learning. Before long, I began to read more than just my homework during these mental workouts. When one of our history books examined the Greek philosophers, I studied them on my own. Soon I was asking myself the great questions of humankind: *What is the soul? What is consciousness? Why are we here? What is the purpose of life?*

When I mentioned these questions to my father, he shook his head with disdain. After his experience of fleeing the region that became Pakistan, he hated religions of all kinds and considered these questions to be at the core of religious thought. "Go to the books that can answer these questions for you," he said. "I have nothing valuable to add." So on my own I read the Bible and the Quran and the Gita, and other Hindu holy scriptures. I eventually became so taken by these works that I secretly decided to become a monk in the Himalayas.

Early one morning I took a bus to the Himalayas, where I presented myself to the abbot at Ramakrishna ashram, a Hindu monastery. "I want to become a holy man," I told him, "a monk."

The abbot listened patiently and then told me it was not my time to become a holy man. When I begged him, he laughed the unfettered laugh of a monk and told his secretary to feed me and give me a place to sleep. The next day he gave me the spiritual initiation of a layperson and sent me back home to Delhi.

When my father discovered what I had done, he was hurt and angry.

"I don't understand," he said. "To become a monk means you would become dead to your family. Why would you want to be dead to your family?"

He was correct. New monks are given a name and new possessions, and their old possessions are burned on a funeral pyre. It is symbolic of the new life they have chosen and means that they will no longer have contact with their birth family.

"You would never get to see us again," said my father. "Why is that appealing to you?"

I couldn't begin to explain why to my father. It wasn't in fact the family I wanted to get away from, just him. Although I was then in medical school, I was still living at home. I was tired of walking on eggs for fear he would yell at me, tired of sneaking into the house after school to quietly ask my mother if he was in a good or bad mood before I said, "Hello, Papa." But there was another reason I wanted to leave: I sincerely desired to learn about spiritual truth, a desire I was sure my father could never understand.

And now this! My father is spiritually rescuing me from hell!

I looked at him as I thought this, and when I did, I saw hope. He was the same yet different. He looked like a person who was enlightened by love. He looked like a person who had gazed into the eyes of God. Universal knowledge granted us in the afterlife allowed me to see and feel him in this new way.

I looked into his eyes, and my hard heart melted in love. I saw a man who was truly at peace.

There were no words that came from his mouth. Rather, information came to me from him telepathically, in an instant.

For the first time, I knew his father had abused him as he had abused us. Visions of his anguish as a child came into my mind as I felt his pain at being brutally beaten as well.

The need to punish all seems so petty, I thought.

Anger always is, said my father. *Anger isn't usually about an event. It's passed on from father to son. If you know that, you can stop it; you can choose not to be angry.*

I could see his father with him, younger and stronger than I remembered as a child. He too had the look of God in his eyes. He did not frown at my father's revelation about the family tradition of anger. He confirmed it with a nod, and for a moment I could feel the pain in his life too. I knew that behind him was a chain of ancestors, each of whom had been filled with anger by their fathers. I also felt their presence somewhere around me, exuding understanding and empathy for the generation behind them who had given them the disease of anger.

But now I felt empathy *from* my father.

Don't pass the anger to your sons, he communicated.

I looked with shame at my father, who returned the look with love and kindness. *I have become the worst of my father as he was the worst of his.* That thought came to me in a flash and with it came a stream of moments in which I had chosen anger over rational behavior.

Will I return to the living? I asked myself. *If I do, I have to focus on love. I have to break the cycle of anger in my family.*

I looked at my father. Without moving his lips, he spoke a truth I will never forget, words clearly from the divine realm: *My son, if you are truthful to your own self, the God, the Divine, the Universe, will take care of you.*

I remembered the last time I saw him alive on earth, that day decades earlier in California when he lay on his deathbed after heart surgery. He was struggling for breath, hoping to live just a little while longer. He was given morphine to take the edge off his painful last moments. The last contact I had with him was touching his feet as he lay dying.

Now I was facing him in the afterlife, a man at peace with himself, a man who had learned the universal truth: love is all there is. He walked me away from hell to a tunnel that teemed with faces from my past—not just my recent past but a past in which I had not been present, the past of my father, and his father, and his father and so on. Around me was a gauntlet of ancestors welcoming me to walk among them to a different realm.

I was pulled into the tunnel, moved forward by their welcoming hands. I turned to thank my father for bringing me here, but he was gone.

Chapter 6

Tunnel of Understanding

As I moved through the tunnel and my ancestors touched me, I experienced parts of their lives telepathically, parts that they wanted to leave with me.

Information came through their touch. It was like flipping channels on a television set. I could see images but couldn't catch the plot.

As I moved forward toward a very bright light, a hand gripped my arm and stopped me. It was my paternal grandfather. He looked into my eyes with great kindness, but the images I received from his touch weren't kind at all.

The incident he showed me was on the night of my birth as my mother proudly held me. I could see that only members of her family surrounded her. My father, *her husband,* was not there.

He was on an education trip he was forced to take for air traffic control schooling. And my grandfather, *the man who now stood before me with a smile on his face*, was not there either. Neither was my grandmother or anyone else from my father's family. Because my grandfather was angry with my father, he forbade anyone from his family from visiting my mother in the hospital. *So petty*, I thought.

I felt mother's sadness that her husband and his family did not share her joyful first day of having a son. I felt my grandfather's petty anger toward my father from that day nearly fifty years ago and also the sorrow he now felt for such small-minded behavior at a time when there should have been so much joy.

Looking at my grandfather now in the tunnel made it difficult for me to imagine that he had ever acted in such a way toward his son's family. He looked young and free of anger or trouble, as those who had transcended their life on earth tended to be. He looked at me with sorrow at the numerous times he had been mean to my father, yet at the same time, he gave a look of sheer joy at apologizing for his trespasses.

Love is the most important thing there is, my grandfather communicated to me. *I am glad to let you know that simple truth while you can still make change in your earthly life.*

My father suddenly appeared next to his father, he too with a look of bliss. He placed his hand on mine, and another painful scene from my childhood appeared.

It was a Sunday, my father's day off, and I asked him to take me to visit my grandparents. He had a headache, he said, and was unable to drive me to their house.

Not wanting to risk his wrath, I sneaked out the back door and walked the five miles to their home, something an eight-year-old should not do, especially in India, where children are often kidnapped. When I arrived, my father was sitting on the couch waiting for me. He had taken his scooter and arrived first.

His face turned red when he saw me. Grabbing me by the arm, he spanked me hard all the way to the scooter while scolding me for my disrespect and disobedience. I remember him saying, "Never do that again. This is a dangerous city for a little boy!"

Though this appeared to be another outburst of anger, it wasn't. Given that I could perceive my father's emotions, I was surprised to also realize how alarmed he had been about my safety. When he discovered I had left the house and gone to my grandparents on my own, he quickly got on his scooter and searched the route for me. When he couldn't find me, he drove to his parents, hoping that I would appear. *He really was concerned for my well-being. He just showed it with anger instead of love*, I thought.

It dawned on me why my father had chosen to show me this simple yet significant event. He wanted it known that he had never been taught any emotion other than anger. I recalled how, when I was older, I learned that my grandfather had often physically abused my father. My father claimed that neither his mother nor father showed him any affection but instead criticized him for his dark skin and unattractive features.

They taught this anger, accepted it, he told me telepathically. *You don't have to pass it on. Simple love is the most important thing in the universe. Love is the best way to discipline because gentleness inspires respect.*

Once again my father and grandfather faded away, leaving me deeply confused. They had shown me thoughtless acts of anger that scarred deeply, yet they now smiled with sorrow, as if to apologize to me. They were showing their greatest faults yet asking forgiveness at the same time, an attitude rarely seen. It was beautiful.

I was able to feel all points of view—mine, my father's and grandfather's, my mother's—that led me to feel all of my emotions. The experience was exhausting yet amazingly healing.

How should I interpret these revelations of anger from my father and grandfather? The answer that came to me from my father was a simple one: *We all have reason to be angry—or not. Anger is a choice.*

That was the second time I had been warned about anger. Both times I thought of my son and our uneasy relationship. *Will I have a chance to right this wrong? Will I have a chance to prevent the anger from being passed down to my son, and then his son?* I asked the question out loud but received no answer.

I was beyond the hands of my ancestors now, maybe halfway through the tunnel. My father and grandfather were gone, and when I looked back to see if they were there, I could see the crowd of ancestors behind me, waving me on. I looked ahead. With no telepathic input from my ancestors, my life review took a pleasant turn. Childhood events that were steeped in kindness, innocence, and fun appeared before me. I relived being with my mother and feeling how much she loved me. We share the same birthday, August 11. Every year, my father would jokingly ask her on our birthday, "What else do you want for a present, I gave you a son?" Her love led her to sometimes spoil me, and in spite of his jokes on her birthday, my father's sternness toward me might have been driven, in part, by jealousy.

From the afterlife, I again saw how wisely my mother nurtured my two younger sisters and me, inspiring our curiosity about the outside world with trips to fairs, boat club events, and to Sapru House to see children's movies. When my sisters were small, my mother and I sometimes shared a still greater adventure, sneaking out of the house and catching the number six bus to the Regal Cinema in downtown New Delhi to see a movie. The high point of many of those days was an ice cream treat. As dangerous as New Delhi was, I remember how safe I felt simply walking with her through the city.

Every evening, she sat with all three of us for evening prayers. A living example of love, compassion, and kindness, she laid the foundation for our dreams and character, advising us about how to behave at home and in the world.

As the eldest child of three and the only son in an Indian family, I have to admit that my sisters spoiled me as much as my mother did. When I ran out of money for sweets, my sisters shared their allowance with me so that I would not be left out. And though I never repaid them, they included me in their games and let me play with their friends as well.

Their courage and generosity were boundless. They also often protected me from my father's wrath, taking the blame and suffering the consequences for what I might have done. Fearing that I might go hungry when I announced my intention to run away to become a monk, my sisters again pooled their pocket money to support me on the journey.

More of those simple moments passed before me, from the unfettered joy of playing with childhood friends to the thrill of learning important lessons in medical school that would later save lives.

These moments were simple delights from my childhood that I now relived knowing how much my mother loved me. *The simple moments are most important,* came a telepathic message from God. More words came to me from the universe: *The simple moments are the most important because there are no simple moments. All moments are memory and lessons. They all build the person you are.*

Another vivid act of kindness unfolded in my mind. It was 1980, and I was in Munich, Germany, to take an exam that would allow me to accept a residency in the United States. After taking the exam, I sat down to watch some street performers downtown. Suddenly I realized I didn't have the booklet that carried my passport. Without it, I would not be able to exchange money or check into a hotel. I might even be arrested or kicked out of the country. I had not made a copy of my passport and didn't know what to do.

I stopped a man who looked like me and asked, "Sir, are you an Indian?"

"No," he replied. "I'm a Pakistani."

I stepped back involuntarily. We Indians and Pakistanis had fought three wars since independence, the last one only a few years before, in 1971. These were wars of religion that we continue to fight on our borders. My father's stories about his escape from Pakistan had also created a bad taste in my mouth for Muslims. The last thing I needed after losing my passport was harassment by a "Paki."

I must have looked deeply troubled because the man then asked what had happened and if he could help. I abruptly told him no.

I started to walk away, but he came to me again. "You seem to be in trouble," he said. "Are you sure I can't help you?"

I felt I had no choice, and he seemed genuine. I told him what the situation was, and he took me to his house where I met his family, who gave me food and shelter. He was an engineer and made a few calls, telling me that he knew what to do in cases of lost passports. He took the next day off work and showed me the highlights of Munich—I still remember visiting the old Olympic Stadium with him. When we returned, the police had found my passport, and I was soon on my way.

These events changed my attitude toward Pakistanis, and even led me to hire one in my Bakersfield pain management practice after I had rejected him initially for being Muslim. *Look beyond labels*, I told myself after the kindness shown to me in Munich by a stranger.

I relived these events in Munich with the same attitude I'd had at the time. But more than that, I felt the goodness of my Pakistani host in his heart at helping a desperate traveler, one he knew had suspicions about his motives.

The voice came into my head again. *We are all born naked and the same. It is later we acquire pride and prejudice . . .*

. . . And anger and addiction and ego and fears, I thought to my telepathic friend. *What happened to me? Why have I become so self-centered? Why do I care more about things than people? It was more than physical pain that led me to become addicted to pain pills, but what was it?* My mind was suddenly searching for answers to questions it had never pondered before, questions that I should have asked when I was still inside that body on the operating table. *What took me so long?*

I could see the Light at the end of the tunnel. It was bright and powerful like a thousand suns, yet as pleasant and welcoming as a beacon guiding me to nirvana. I worked my way toward the Light, weightless like an astronaut pulling himself along the outside of a spacecraft. The end of the tunnel was overwhelmingly bright, but I was not concerned. There was something about it that pulled me toward it—a sense of mystery, perhaps, or the magnetic pull of pure and true love. I had no fear of the Light. Instead I was thrilled and ready for all the good things I knew were in the core of its brightness.

But my forward motion slowed, then stopped, and then suddenly I realized I was no longer moving forward but backward, backward to another place and time, one where past life events would explain some of my own life's dilemmas.

Chapter 7

Past Life, Future Life

The darkness engulfed me, and out of it came visions of a life I didn't at first recognize but that turned out to be one of my past lives.

In the first vision, I was sitting in a royal courtyard in medieval India, feeling the power of my position as a prince of the region. The scene before me was vivid. The grass was bright green and well kept and lined with tall stone statues of Indian gods and goddesses. In front of those statues were farmers, the farmers who tilled my land and raised crops that made me wealthy.

I was angry, but I don't know why. From my princely perspective, I rose up from my throne and walked toward the farmers, swinging a whip as I moved through the cool grass. I had no fear of retribution or self-defense from the farmers because on either side of me were several loyal soldiers who advanced with me and also swung whips.

I could not remember why I was torturing those who worked so hard for me. Perhaps it was that I didn't think they had worked hard enough or that I was trying to teach them a lesson about my power. Perhaps it had not rained enough for good crops, and I blamed the lack of perfect weather on them. Perhaps it was just for fun. I do not know. I do know that I took great joy in slashing the backs of the farmers after they had fallen to the ground. And I do know that my wrist began to hurt terribly after I administered these beatings, so much so that I couldn't use that hand again without experiencing extreme pain.

As I watched my shameful performance, I flashed forward to my current life where I had experienced a torn ligament in my right wrist. The pain had become so severe that I had taken pain pills to cope with daily life. Why had I recalled the pain in my wrist now?

Was it because I had been so mean to these people, workers who had looked to me for guidance and wisdom yet received the business end of a switch? This was not a question I could answer. I could only watch in shame as I beat these peasants with all my might.

I believe the medieval me was out of control and would not listen to the modern me. But my mind processed what it saw with its new enlightenment, and the new enlightenment was horrified. I could hear a voice speak to me telepathically. He told me in kind yet demanding terms to beg the farmers for forgiveness. I did so without hesitation because I was ashamed at what I saw myself doing.

I was horrible to you, I said as I watched the beatings play out before me. *Forgive me for what I was doing.*

One by one the farmers came to me and accepted my apology, some even touching me to convey human kinship, something they never would have done had they thought I wasn't sincere. When they put their hands on me, I felt a jolt like electricity that rattled me to my very bones. I am sure it was this steady stream of loving jolts that healed the ligament tear in my right wrist that had caused me pain for years. Within months of my near-death experience to the present day, the pain has never been as severe.

As I faded from the life of the medieval prince, many more of my lives flashed before me the way pictures in a picture book would if one were to flip through it very quickly. These lives were vaguely familiar, but as soon as I tried to focus on one, another captured my attention and then another. During this event, I realized that time was not linear. Time could go backward, and it could go in a circular fashion; time could be the past, present, and future all at once. Time is a human invention to cope with our life span, I concluded. But time itself does not exist, at least not in the way we think it does. It is us, our minds, that make our life span into a "time line."

Suddenly the rapid review of lives stopped, and another specific life review began. I found myself sitting at the doorway of a large mud building, gazing out at a green field of plants. There were other houses to one side of the field, and I knew the people who lived there. They were coming out of their mud homes and walking slowly into the fields to perform their day's work. At that point, who and where I was rapidly unfolded in my mind.

I was in a mountain town in Afghanistan in the nineteenth century, and before me was a field of poppies, their green pods sitting atop the stems like Popsicles on a stick. I had inherited this field of poppies from my late father and was now one of the top opium producers in the region. I was making a tremendous amount of money from the sale of these poppies, but my financial status was no longer the focus of my life. Rather, I had fallen in love with my own product. I was an opium addict.

I was presented with several scenes in which I found myself in the field tasting poppy sap from the plants. In the fields, the workers scored the outside of the pods to prepare them for processing, and I walked the rows, smearing the tarlike substance on my fingers and putting it in my mouth. The narcotic buzz I got from the sap was good, but it was nothing compared to the feelings from the final product. The men who processed the sap and produced the drug rolled tiny balls of the stuff for me to smoke in the evening.

In the beginning, it was heavenly to inhale the opium. It put my brain into a state of pleasure that made me feel as though I was floating in warm ocean water, detached from my surroundings. Infused with this evil bliss, I watched the poppy field change color with the sunset and the day pass into night. But the joy of using opium turned to hell when I decided I wanted more. I found myself "testing" the crop all day, every day, telling my employees that I had to test the drug for purity before it went to market.

I knew they knew the truth and also knew that they would eventually move me to a hut and supply product to me that would keep me high all day while stealing the proceeds from my farm. I knew all of this would happen, but I didn't care. I was firmly hooked on the sensations of opium, especially the focus it allowed me to put on me and me alone.

I have been given this addiction again, I thought as I watched my nineteenth-century self smoke the highly addictive opiates. My addiction to modern narcotics was no different from that of the addiction I experienced more than a century earlier. Vicodin or opium, it's all the same. What was different was that I was experiencing it in a past life. *What does that mean?* I asked myself.

It means you now know that your challenges from the past are presented to you again, said the universal voice that was with me telepathically. *You have another life and another chance to cure your addictions.*

I realized that in my current life, I was echoing behavior from my previous lives, behaving with a lack of love to those less fortunate, misusing my material wealth and social status, and numbing myself to real life with painkillers and antidepressants. As this insight pulsed through me, another wave of awareness washed over me: if I were still alive after this surgery, I would have to break these patterns completely and live differently. Perhaps I would be given another chance to conquer my failings.

I was frightened yet thrilled at what had happened so far. Leaving my body and now traveling through this tunnel was like the first time I rode on a roller coaster: I feared the outcome yet wanted more of the experience.

The past life dissolved around me, and I was back in the tunnel again. Ahead was a bright Light and next to me, once again, was my father. He took my hand and led me toward the Light. And as he had before, he repeated the words telepathically that he had communicated to me previously: *"If you keep your consciousness clear and be truthful to yourself, the Universe and the Divine will take care of you."*

His words flooded my entire being. I felt deeply soothed, and had the understanding that in this moment, right now, my life was being redirected.

(As a postscript to this chapter I want to mention that similar past life events also took place during deep meditation sessions occurring under the direction of Brian Weiss, MD, a noted psychiatrist and regression therapist. These therapy sessions are done through hypnosis and have resulted in a number of additional memories that have convinced me not only that we have past lives, but that they are accessible under a variety of transcendent conditions besides NDEs, such as meditation and hypnosis. I use these methods myself to explore further into my past lives.)

Chapter 8

Future Shock

My father led me down the tunnel and toward the Light, and we looked at it together, its intensity oddly soothing. I moved forward and then began to walk rapidly in its direction, pulled by a powerful sense of love emanating from its radiance. My father let go of my hand, and I kept moving forward. As I did so, two angelic forms emerged into the tunnel. They exuded a powerful vigor—a charisma and energy that made them seem magnetic. I approached them with awe as they hovered above me and smiled with joy and confidence. Telepathically they introduced themselves as Michael and Raphael, archangels of the Bible.

Because I had studied the Bible, I was not afraid of these angels. What I could tell from this encounter, however, was that they were powerful spiritual beings and unmistakably angels. It was only with later research I learned that Saint Michael is the protector of people and the angel who opens doors and Saint Raphael is the angel of healers.

They announced that they were my guardian angels, helpers sent to guide people like me who had come over from the other side. In a moment I was lifted by them and guided toward a Being of Light that I could see in the blazing fog of light before me. As we flew toward this Being, the angels carried on a clever banter between themselves and with me, talking telepathically about the beauty of heaven and its effect on the senses of the newly arrived.

If we let you go, you wouldn't know how to move forward, said Michael, as we moved through this weightless atmosphere. *It's like being in water, but there's no way to move forward.*

You have to think yourself forward, said Raphael. *Push yourself with your thoughts.*

Some humans are very good at moving themselves forward with their thoughts, said Michael with a chuckle.

Start thinking or be left behind, laughed Raphael.

The Light was still far away, and as we approached it, we went higher and then into a meadow that was green like emerald stones and peppered with rosebushes, the blooms as red as wine. The sweet smell of grass and roses made me almost delirious with pleasure. A crystal-clear stream of water cut through the meadow, and the air off the distant mountains was blowing gently. Around me in the sky was the deep and gentle sound of "om," as though it were being chanted by nature itself. It sounded primordial.

I closed my eyes and went with my senses, now fully engaged. I have no idea how long my eyes were closed or what I was thinking as they were, other than to say I was in a state of *Shanti,* pure peace, bliss, and love. The angels laughed at me.

Some people who come here are so thrilled they would leave their body if they weren't out of it already, communicated Michael.

They feel something they have never felt before and find something inside they didn't know exists, communicated Raphael. *It takes them to a new place in themselves.*

As we went to a higher plane and then a higher one still, this heavenly realm became more formless, until I was surrounded by a landscape of clear light.

I must have appeared nervous at being in this formless, nameless environment because Michael put his hand on my shoulder as a means of comfort and communicated, *The higher you go up in the spiritual realms, the more formless it becomes.*

Raphael touched my other shoulder, communicating further information. *That's right. You become surrounded by a powerful entity of energy, of pure love and intelligence, and this pure love is the base reality, the underlying fabric, of everything in the universe. It is the source of all creation, the creative force of the universe.*

Yes, communicated Michael, *this pure love is the source of all that makes the universe. It is contained in everything imaginable yet somehow ignored by so many. Enlightenment comes when a person realizes that love is everywhere and is the only thing that matters. Yet most don't reach that realization until they leave the earth. The ones who come back remember the purpose and presence of love in everything. And they remember it the rest of their lives.*

Sometimes they change personality from their exposure to it, communicated Raphael. *Police become like social workers, schoolteachers become spiritual masters, cynical doctors become truly caring caregivers. Love adds dimension to everything.*

It becomes a new form of currency, communicated Michael. *A wealthy person sometimes wants more love than money. They want to give more than receive.*

You'll see, communicated Raphael.

The archangels looked like humans yet at the same time were as far from human as possible. They shimmered with light and had a thick translucence that made them translucent yet solid at the same time. Michael had a blue hue and long hair; Raphael was greenish and wore a cap. Standing amid the atmosphere of pure love, they exuded a power that made me realize they could overwhelm most anything. They had a command of love and a complete knowledge of how it works. For these angels and the others who were certainly present, the atmosphere of pure love was their breath of life, the clean mountain air of heaven.

The angels took me by the arms and we moved rapidly upward toward the Being of Light. The Light became brighter, and as it did, we moved faster and faster. I looked at the angels, and they were in a state of concentration and bliss. As we moved closer to the Being, my guardian angels became so translucent that they nearly disappeared.

Ahead was a silver-blue form that showed no sign of being male or female. This form was large and exuded a familiarity, perhaps it was a member of my family whom I deeply loved. I knew the Being of Light very well, yet at the same time it was new to me. Still, when it took me into its space and engulfed me with its blue Light, I knew I was loved and that it knew more about me than I about it. I was wrapped in its total knowledge.

There was a lot to absorb, a lot to think about. But the Being of Light left me no time to do either. It began gently whispering in my ear. And as the words started, pure love—I don't know what else to call it—pervaded everything, as if my five earthly senses were soaked in omniscient, all-powerful love. The more I became wrapped up with the Being of Light, the more distinct became the chant of "om." I was at once communicating with and in the Being of Light. *I am one with the universe*, I thought.

It seemed as though the universe closed in on me and wrapped itself around me. I was enclosed in the feeling of velvet, comfortable and warm and soft, a living blanket of loving Light that charged me with energy.

The Being of Light closed the door on my old world and created a new one, a world that I could never have conjured for myself, a new world that keeps unfolding and unfolding with new aspects and discoveries every day and that drive me even now. The Being of Light opened a Pandora's box that contained all good instead of evil. But like anything else new, that good took time to navigate.

As I was wrapped securely in a blanket of pure love, the Being of Light communicated telepathically. *You need to look at your life one more time,* it said. *It's important to reflect on changes that you need to make.*

With that, I had another painful life review that reminded me of things I had done or thought for which I was not proud. One event took place in medical school in India. Medical school was extremely difficult and as a result very competitive. We competed with our grades, trying to push ourselves higher in the rankings while trying to push one another down by almost any method possible.

Such was the case with one of the students in my dorm. He worked at his studies as hard as anyone else, and he was also smarter by nature. Those of us who ranked below him in grades were not happy at having him in our class.

He too was apparently not happy for emotional reasons. Out of personal anguish that was a mystery to us all, this young man committed suicide by jumping out of his third-floor dorm room.

Now, in my life review, I recalled the event as I had heard it from one student and then another as the story was told in bits and pieces. What bothered me now, however, was not so much that the young man had killed himself. I had nothing to do with that. What bothered me was that so many of us were pleased that there would be one fewer student to compete with.

When the life review finished, I was ashamed. Although it was in no way a total review of my life, I was steeped in the pain of my selfishness and the way I had made others feel or the way I had felt about others. I realized that I had not reached out enough to help alleviate pain in others, especially those I thought were beneath me. Worst of all, I had not considered the needs of my son. I had forced him to go to medical school without taking into consideration what he wanted for his own life. *My life has been for only me.* I hadn't cared enough for my fellow human beings.

I felt small and full of shame and expected the Being of Light to do . . . *what?* Shake my soul? Vaporize me? Send me to hell? I had no idea what to expect. But rather than receiving something bad, I felt a deep sense of love coming from the Being of Light, the kind of love I should have exhibited with my son.

Everything will be all right for you, said the Being of Light, telling me that soon I would return to my earthly life. But there would be a change, said the Being. *Now you will become a healer of the soul.*

I was not clear on what it meant to become a "healer of the soul," but the Being quickly filled in the knowledge gap. *I am talking about diseases of the soul,* said the Being. *These are problems like addiction, depression, and chronic pain.*

My life would now focus on healing the diseases I'd had and therefore knew them personally.

First came the cancer, said the Being, *and along with that came increasing depression, often caused by an overwhelming fear of disability and death. Chronic pain followed the cancer surgery, and with it the disability and exhaustion that come from jolts of pain when one moves in the wrong way or the nagging aches that keep one from ever being totally comfortable or sleeping soundly. You have experienced these,* said the Being. *These are diseases that tax the soul. Since you know them well, you will show other people how to fight these diseases spiritually.*

In order to do this, the Being of Light revealed my new path. I would no longer be an anesthesiologist. Instead I would become a practitioner of spiritual medicine, a practitioner of consciousness-based healing. Instead of putting people to sleep, I would now focus on waking them up.

I was neither shocked nor surprised that I was to make a change in my life. The Being of Light was powerful and wise, and I knew that I would accept whatever was revealed to be the pillar of my future life. But still something the Being of Light said had left me feeling uncomfortable. *What is consciousness-based healing?* I asked. *How do I practice something if I don't know what it is?*

The Being was patient. It told me that consciousness-based healing is the treatment of diseases through spiritual means. A wearing down of the spirit causes many diseases, and people then turn to drugs, or alcohol, or bad behavior in a misguided effort to regain their spiritual strength.

Those substances and behaviors don't work, said the Being. *People keep trying to build their spirit by taking more substances or practicing behaviors like control over others, expressing extreme anger, or having excessive sex for reasons other than love. Even when they know these substances and bad behaviors aren't working, they continue to use them because they have now become addicted. When that happens, the spirit can wear away to nothing.*

It takes one to know one, I told myself. *Because I have had the problems, I can be better equipped to treat them.*

The Being of Light laughed telepathically when it heard what I was thinking. And it told me that, yes, because of my own addictions and the enlightenment, and the energy transmission I was now receiving, I was ready to move into the realm of spiritual medicine.

Now it is time to be healer of the soul, especially of the diseases of soul, like addiction, depression, and chronic pain.

The Being was repeating what it had said before, perhaps to emphasize its plan or perhaps because the idea of making change in my life was so foreign to me that I could not connect with this new way of practicing a healing art and this new way of living.

Show me what you mean, I asked.

The Being of Light backed away for a moment and then wrapped itself tightly around me. Colors of the prism arose and fell until a blue-gray color presented itself. I could see a man deep in meditation who was clearly gaining valuable wisdom from the archangels Michael and Raphael. Light and dark passed quickly over the man as though the sun were rising and setting, which I took to mean that he was spending many hours meditating because all of it was valuable time well spent. As the man came into focus, I could see that he was me.

The perspective continued, and I could see myself growing in spiritual wisdom with each passing minute of meditation. It was as though I was taking steps into new realms of wisdom, learning more about the challenges all humans have to enlightenment and how to address them. I could see my flaws in painful detail, and as I meditated, I could see how to confront those flaws and take them out of my life without guilt and recrimination. As I continued the meditations, I could see how to teach others what I was learning.

I slipped into the vision, seeing through my own eyes instead of watching myself in the third person. As I did, I was standing in front of hundreds of people, telling them about my brush with heaven and what I learned about life from my voyage to hell and my brief exposure to this marvelous Being of Light. That I was not afraid as I spoke to them surprised me. The thought of speaking to hundreds of people should have horrified me as it always had before. *I'm an anesthesiologist. I don't like to speak to people!* The truth was that like most other people, I would rather be dead than speak in public.

It'll be fine, said the Being of Light. *Your life is going to change. You are going to change.*

As the Being made this proclamation, another image appeared. I was in a clinic, one with no walls and bright natural light streaming through the windows. On the floor in various poses were patients performing yoga, and in another part of the clinic were a few rows of people sitting in cross-legged meditation poses, each looking blissful as he or she concentrated on gaining spiritual information from the universe.

I knew that almost everyone in the clinic had been seriously ill, if not with a physical illness like cancer, then with the illness of drug or alcohol addiction. The people I saw in this clinic had made the choice to confront their illness and absolve their pain with natural methods, primarily meditation. It was clearly more of a battle for some of them than for others, but I was gratified to know that most were winning and doing it with the holistic methods I was teaching them.

This is consciousness-based healing, said the Being of Light. *This is what you must learn and teach. This is your new life.*

Exactly what is consciousness-based healing? I asked. *Give me the knowledge. Teach it to me.*

You have the knowledge, said the Being of Light. *You have been humbled by pain, so you have the knowledge. But you must teach yourself. Finding the knowledge inside you is the best way to learn. If you don't learn for yourself, you will not learn completely.*

You'll have us to help you, said Raphael, who was now behind me with Michael. *We will be with you when you want us to be. We can guide you.* But also you now have the gift of directing healing energy, and you have medical intuition.

I don't know how long I was with the Being. I do know that I was given a period of reflection after hearing of my new mission in life. I also know that the Being gave me more information, but I don't remember what it was, or at least I didn't remember it at the time. It came to me later when I needed it, and I was glad it did, because there is nothing like a spiritual transformation to make one feel alone. I can now say that my road to spiritual enlightenment is a lonely one because it has changed me into someone else.

Eventually I moved away from the Being of Light. I had been completely revealed to the Being and felt uncomfortable in my emotional nakedness. I felt the pain of honest reflection, and frankly I expected serious rebuke and possibly even a threat or two from the Being.

But that didn't happen. Rather, I felt a blast of love from the Being of Light, one I would need to make it through the coming years of catharsis and confusion. I felt a tremendous sense of gratitude for this love that surrounded me. The Being clearly understood all, especially that none of us is perfect. It gave me another chance to reconfigure my life into one that was a little more perfect so that I could help my fellow human beings.

In retrospect, I think the Being of Light might have been Jesus, but I have no way of truly knowing. I do know that it was a cosmic consciousness of some kind, one that grants us understanding and institutes positive human change. If it wasn't Jesus, it was some other Being that loves us, understands our weaknesses, and helps us develop new intentions. Perhaps that was all I needed to know.

I could feel myself move rapidly away from the Being of Light and fall into a field of whiteness that was like plummeting through fluffy white clouds. I felt revived, reborn, a man with a new plan, *a man with a mission! I was going to change the world and my relationship to everything in it!*

I would have been glad to stay in the heavenly realm, but now I was ready to return and introduce the world to the new Raj. I felt a little elated and a bit frightened. I felt as though I was about to spend my first day on earth.

Chapter 9

Caught by Karma

I felt as though I was driving very fast through a bright-white fog on a road I could not see. The drive was horrifying and exhilarating at the same time, horrifying because I feared I might slam into something and be killed on the roadside, yet exhilarating because I knew I was not driving at all but accelerating through the universe.

In retrospect I realize it made no difference how I felt. I had no control over my voyage, not from the beginning when I left my body in the operating room until now as I zoomed toward the next destination. The universe had taken over and was in complete control of all aspects of my life. I was just a spectator.

Is that how it's always been? I wondered as I zoomed through the fog. *Has the universe always controlled my life and I just thought I was in charge?*

As I pondered the events that had passed and wondered what was coming next, I noticed that I seemed to decelerate, and as I did, the fog became brighter and my eyes began to hurt. I closed my eyes to shield them from the brightness, and when I opened them, I was in the recovery room.

My heart was beating hard and my lungs pumping double time as I tried to suck in all of the cool air I could. I had just completed the experience of my life—or was it death?—and everything that had happened was vivid in my brain and struggling to get out.

"How do you feel?"

I looked above me to see the anesthesiologist. Being one myself, I knew that he would be the first of the surgical staff to visit. He was still in his scrubs and had his surgical mask dangling across his shoulder in a dramatic way. His smile was Hollywood bright.

"That was a rough one," he said, referring to my surgery.

I said nothing, but I don't think he noticed. He told me about the difficulty they had experienced during my surgery and said that "certain events" had presented challenges for the surgeons and proved to be "at times very alarming."

I must have looked stunned, because when I didn't respond, he leaned closer.

"Are you all right?" he asked.

"I saw you during my surgery," I said.

"Really," he said, his smile fading.

"Yes. I left my body and watched you from the ceiling."

"Of course," he said, breezing through my medical file as though there was some clue in there as to why I left my body.

"Interesting," he said, his voice a study in disinterest.

"No really. I watched as you administered the anesthetic and even heard you tell a joke."

"Oh really. And what was the joke?"

I recalled it for him, the ribald joke that made the surgeon and operating room staff laugh. The anesthesiologist blushed when I told the joke.

"I must not have given you enough anesthesia," he said, looking doubly hard at the file to avoid my gaze.

"No, you gave me plenty," I replied, recounting the amount of medication I had seen him administer.

The doctor emitted the kind of pained cough one might emit when receiving certain types of examinations. I could tell he was uncomfortable.

"I saw a lot more when I was out of my body," I said.

I told him about going to India where I saw my mother and sister plan their evening meal and how my late father rescued me on the cusp of hell. I started to tell him more, but he glanced at his watch and flipped the file closed.

"Very interesting," he said. "I'll come back later to hear about it."

I never saw him again.

He was not the only one. When the surgeon came to visit, I recounted my out-of-body journey and got all the way to the tunnel entrance before he reached for his phone (which was not ringing) and excused himself by faking an "important call." A resident came in, and I cornered him with questions about consciousness-based healing. He struggled to define it, but when I told him two Christian angels and a Being of Light I met while on the operating table presented the concept to me, he too lost his enthusiasm for further conversation. Had I told him it was a new form of medicine developed by a major medical institution, I'm sure he would have maintained the discussion for a long time.

More attuned to this subject were the nurses. They spend quality time with the patients and hear experiences like these in "real time," as one nurse said. It is not uncommon for patients to awaken from their surgical slumber and tell nurses of encounters with departed loved ones or mysterious Beings of Light. When this happens, said one nurse, a simple check of their medical records usually reveals a cardiac arrest or some other brush with death while on the operating table.

"They've had what is called a near-death experience," said the nurse, who went on to describe the phenomenon as being "the time when a person becomes aware that they have died because they leave their body."

Of course I knew what a near-death experience was. The few medical books that mention the phenomenon describe it as a subjective experience that people report after the threat of nearly dying or from actually "being in death." Near-death experiences (NDEs) generally involve leaving one's body, seeing dead relatives, having a life review, meeting angelic Beings of Light, and so on. And because I am an anesthesiologist, I am usually the first in the surgical team to hear about it from the patient. But up to this point, I had also been the first on the surgical team to ignore the patient's experience. As I was with "the frozen man" in the introduction to this book, so was I with all the other patients who reported "personal anomalies."

As I lay in recovery, I remembered other events I had ignored. In one incident, a patient awoke to tell me he had left his body only moments before and traveled down the hall to a waiting room, where he witnessed a very stressed-out woman talking angrily at her child and a man in a bright orange shirt reading a newspaper. The patient spoke excitedly about this supposed adventure out of body. It would have taken me less than a minute to walk down the hall to the waiting room to see if what he thought he saw was true. *Why had I not gone to see if such a scene truly existed?* Other patients reported "unearthly lights" and "strange dreams" involving departed family members. *Was I really too busy to ask further questions, or did I just not care?*

I certainly cared now. I was not happy with the doctors who had ignored and even mocked my experience. *I am a medical doctor and deserve a higher level of respect,* I said to myself. I was a veteran medical doctor, one trained to make medical observations. I knew what I experienced. I was certain of all the events because I observed them firsthand. *Why am I being challenged?* I realized at that point that I had usually been the one who had challenged patients when they tried to talk about their NDEs. Now the glove was on the other hand, and I didn't like the way it felt.

Now I wished I had been more curious about this phenomenon, readier to talk to patients about their experience and even done the simple legwork to see if what they thought they saw when they left their bodies was indeed true.

Despite my dissatisfaction with the way my colleagues treated me, I knew what had happened. I was a victim of karma. In other words, you sow what you reap.

I was reaping my karma now, that was for sure. Surprisingly, though, I believed I deserved it and would learn from it in the end. An old Indian saying seemed appropriate now as well as funny: *There is nothing like a hard butt in the head to make you aware of the goat.* I laughed as I repeated it. *I know what I saw. I have nothing to fear from the truth.*

Chapter 10

Merry Christmas

I had been in recovery about two hours when Arpana came in. She knew I'd had a difficult surgery from the surgeon who talked to her in the waiting room and was surprised to see me in an animated conversation with one of the nurses.

When I saw Arpana, I shifted my attention to her. I told her as rapidly as I could about my experience, practically spewing out the events as though I was afraid she would declare me insane when she heard what had happened.

She listened patiently to the events of my near-death experience. She appeared nervous when I told her of leaving my body and frightened when I described my close encounter with hell. Yet she nearly laughed when she heard of my happiness at seeing my father because she knew our relationship had not been cordial. And the past life experience got but a nod because past lives are a pillar of the Hindu religion. But when I told her about being greeted by the two Christian saints, Michael and Raphael, she stopped me in my tracks.

"Wait a minute. You are Hindu. What happened to the fifty thousand gods and goddesses in our religion?" she asked. "Why weren't they there to help you?"

I paused for a moment and shrugged. *I had not been a devoted Hindu except for the short time I wished to be a monk. Why was I now being helped by saints from another religion?* The question baffled me and left me only with another question that would have to be answered.

I could tell from the uneasy look on Arpana's face that there were many questions yet to be answered for her too. She was clearly uneasy at what I was telling her. She showed embarrassment at times and shrugged nervously at others. By the time I finished talking, she seemed not to recognize the man she had been married to for twenty-two years.

"What does all this mean?" she said in a loud whisper.

"It means big changes for us," I said.

"Like . . . ?"

"Raphael says I must now talk to patients about healing their spirit," I said.

Arpana laughed.

"Raja, you don't like to talk to patients. That's why you became an anesthesiologist. How are you going to make that change?"

The question made me feel uneasy, so I ignored it. That I did not like talking to patients was true. I often considered it a waste of time and felt that most patients didn't listen anyway. *How am I going to adjust my attitude?*

"The angels told me that I now need to practice a new form of medicine, something they call consciousness-based healing."

"What's that?" Arpana asked patiently.

"I don't know," I admitted. "I think it's medicine that heals the spirit, a kinder form of medicine that helps the patient heal without using too many drugs. Perhaps it has to do with integrating yoga or meditation or other modalities that elevate consciousness. Maybe it's more than that. I just don't know yet. I just know that there are many changes. I am going to be on a different path. The angels have told me."

"What is the path?" asked Arpana, her questions becoming as direct and focused as her eyes, which I now tried to avoid.

"I have to quit being an anesthesiologist and search for the path. It is out there. I just need to find it."

I saw a mix of worry and excitement in Arpana's eyes, the look of someone seeing an unexplored new frontier clearly filled with challenge and excitement. *Is that really what I saw?* I looked again and now saw the face of a frightened wife, one who was realizing this man in bed was clearly not the husband she had brought to surgery just the day before.

"What day is it?" I asked her.

"Yesterday was Christmas," she said.

"Merry Christmas," I said.

We made small talk for several minutes, avoiding conversation about the events of my near-death experience and especially the new life that the angels had plotted out for us. At one point Arpana asked what my father looked like, and I choked with emotion, telling her that he looked thirty years younger than the day he had died and, best of all, he was free of anger. She just smiled and nodded after that but couldn't seem to squeeze any words out.

––––––––––

The surgical wounds across my stomach were open so the infection that remained could ooze out onto the bandages. Leaving the surgical site open is necessary to make sure infection doesn't get trapped inside the body and begin to fester again. The downside is that the nerve endings are exposed to air and become very sensitive. Every time I moved, gauze covering the wound would irritate the nerve endings, and I would get a jolt of excruciating pain.

I tried to smile and talk my way through the pain, but it soon became obvious to the nurse on duty that I needed more narcotics. She injected more morphine into the IV tube that ran into my arm, and before long I felt the heavy curtain of sleep come over my eyes.

Chapter 11

The Ladder of Enlightenment

Many patients who have near-death experiences forget them shortly after they occur. This can often happen as a result of anesthesia, especially the type that creates forgetfulness as part of its effect.

I have seen this myself in patients who have heart surgery and are given a cocktail of anesthesia to make the experience as painless as possible. One man in particular came back to consciousness in the recovery room and told me and several family members around his bedside about being greeted by his late father who soothed him through the long surgery by walking with him through a verdant landscape he called heaven. His family listened in awe as he described the walk and all that he saw. I listened with mild patience, hoping he would finish the story quickly so I could get on with my rounds. Finally, tired of waiting, I ordered a shot of Haldol be given to him because I thought he was having delusions. The next day, when I asked him about his walk in heaven, he could not remember the event at all.

In a way, I hoped the narcotics would make me forget and I wouldn't have to carry out the transformation that now seemed to be my destiny. But that didn't happen. When I awoke several hours later, I was in a private room with the IV bag still hanging over me and the sharp pain of the surgical wounds throbbing across my abdomen. Arpana was asleep on an uncomfortable chair in the corner of the room, and events of my near-death experience were with me as clearly as if they had just happened.

I was of two minds about this persistence of memory. I didn't want to make changes in my life because staying on my given path would be easier despite the stress of overwork and the pain of my illness and addiction. Still, the door had been opened, and I had been shown a new way of life by Beings that to this day I can only describe as angels. To have forgotten the experience would be the easy way out. But now I realized the memory of the experience was here to stay, and for that reason, my life would now take a new path, one with many obstacles to avoid and puzzles to solve. Oddly, I felt joy.

_____

I was watching Arpana curled up in the uncomfortable chair, her face against her knees. Her slow, rhythmic breathing seemed to indicate she was in a deep sleep, but when I looked at her eyes, I realized she was looking at me.

I tried to be funny.

"There are other gifts from the angels that I want to share with you," I said.

She raised her head but did not lower her knees. Instead she wrapped her arms around her shins and kept them in front of her, looking the way teenagers do when they are trying to protect themselves from their parents' words.

She said nothing.

"I saw my life in a way I've never seen before," I said. "When I stood next to hell, I realized I had led a self-centered and materialistic life. It has always been all about the possessions, Arpana. My whole life has been about supporting material objects—the house, cars, vacations."

Even my choice of medical specialty. I remembered how I had trained to be a pediatrician when I first arrived in the United States. Even going so far as to pass the pediatric board exams. But I was not happy with the amount of money pediatricians make, which happens to be the lowest paid specialty in American medicine. So I explored to find out which medical specialty makes the most money and then did another residency in anesthesiology, among the top earning physicians. Later, to increase my income, I opened a pain management clinic. Between my hospital job and the clinic, I was working sixty to eighty hours a week.

"What about us?" she interrupted. "What about your family?"

"I am proud of my family, but I can't enjoy it when my whole life is a struggle to support materialism. I never thought I wanted it any other way, but now I know I've been on the wrong path."

"I wouldn't say you've never wanted it any other way," she said. Her knees came down, and her feet were firmly planted on the floor. She leaned forward and said nothing, but I knew from her hurt and angry stare exactly what she was referring to. My life had been filled with materialistic mistakes.

Things went fine until they didn't. In retrospect, I can say only that the stock market resembles life in that it is controlled by forces we often can't control, anticipate, or understand. What was supposed to be a mountain of profit turned into a pit of debt and depression as the market crashed and, with it, all of the money I had invested. All of it. By the end of my disastrous investing career, I had lost all of the invested money and then some. I was more than broke. I was broken.

I had gone about the process of rebuilding, but it was slow. Too slow. I apologized to all of the family members I had borrowed money from, but the humiliation was immense. I realized what I should have known from the beginning: that because I was a good doctor didn't mean I was a good investor. I realized something else too: greed is not always good.

The depression associated with such failure was astounding. That is what my wife was referring to now. As I saw the look on her face, a horrible incident came back to me, one that took place several months after the loss of the investment. I was still deeply depressed from the loss, and she was trying her best to bring me out of it with a cheerful subject.

"What would you like for your birthday, Raja?" she had asked.

I blurted out the only thing on my mind.

"I would like for you to let me go, put me behind you. I would like permission to die and for you and our family to go on without me."

I had even thought about how I would commit suicide. Being an anesthesiologist, I had access to all of the medications necessary to make a clean exit from this world. But the look in Arpana's eyes told me I had no right to think about a "clean exit" from this world. She was deeply hurt by what I had said.

"Shame on you," she said. "To even think such a thing is selfish and self-centered. Don't you care about your family? To leave us without you and alone? We would not recover from the loss!"

She had never forgotten that moment. She was remembering it now as she sat in the hospital chair and gave me the same look she had given me on that day.

Suddenly I realized what she was thinking. *She thinks I want to die! She thinks I want to go to the other side and leave the family!*

"Arpana, no!" I said. "I don't want to die! I want to live! I want us all to live!"

She settled back in the chair as I struggled to raise myself a little higher in the hospital bed.

"I have so much to tell you," I said. "It is all about our life and how to have a more meaningful existence."

I began with the angels, Michael and Raphael, and the information they gave me on the way to see the Being of Light about levels of consciousness and healing.

"I am currently at the lowest level," I told Arpana. "Michael defined that level as being one that is very materialistic and unenlightened."

"What did they say?" asked Arpana.

Their comments were so clear in my mind that I was able to recall the conversation almost word for word that we had on the way to the Being of Light.

"Most of what you purchase in the materialistic world is really nothing more than tools to make your life easier or more pleasant," I said, quoting Michael.

"Yes, things like houses and cars are tools for a better life," Raphael had said. "That is how they are supposed to be used. But your tools are fancy, big, and ridiculous, and they cost so much that you aren't using them; they are using you. They are causing you to have a sick ego. And the worst is that you don't own your possessions; they own you!"

"Right," said Michael. "And the sad thing is that nobody really cares about your materialistic possessions. They care only about their own. It is only your ego that cares, and nothing can torment a person at a low level of consciousness more than an ego that is sick.

"Breaking the bonds of materialism will bring you to a higher level," said Michael. "And after that you will move up through the levels by being a loving person and helping others. The more you help others, the more you help yourself."

"Yes, it's called the ladder of enlightenment," said Raphael. "The more you help others, the higher up in enlightenment you can climb. Goodness to others makes you more enlightened."

Arpana's face softened. I couldn't yet tell if she believed in the events of my NDE, but she most certainly liked the idea of a more enlightened husband.

"When I asked them how to get to the highest level, both angels pointed to the Being of Light that was ahead of us," I said to Arpana.

"You will experience the highest level in a moment, as soon as you reach the Light," said Michael. "It is like everything and nothing. And you will never forget it."

"It's like a black hole," said Raphael, a comment that made both of the angels laugh as though a very funny joke had been told.

"I could not tell if the Being of Light was male or female, or any sex at all," I told Arpana. The brightness of the Light kept me from seeing it, if there was truly an "it" to be seen. Rather, I was absorbed into the Light and was completely comfortable in its brightness and the feeling of it, which seemed to tingle with energy.

"I wanted to become a part of the Being of Light," I told Arpana. "I didn't want to come back to my life, but it was made clear to me immediately that I would be going back and that everything would be all right for me, but that a lot would change."

"Like what?" she asked.

"Let me put it this way: the Being of Light tore me apart and put me together again as a new person, one who was dying to wake up," I said. "It told me the dangers of leading a soulless and materialistic life. It told me I had been very uncaring toward my patients and said I needed to advance beyond just excellent technical skill and into human skills. To do that, I will have to give up anesthesiology and become a healer of the soul. It said my suffering has already given me some training to help those with diseases of the soul. Once I learn how to handle the depression, chronic pain, and addiction in my own life, I will be suited to help others. It said I have had to suffer these things in my own life so I can develop empathy for these conditions and become a healer of the soul. It said I must search for the meaning of this sentence: *The healing of these diseases can only be achieved through consciousness.* When I can understand that sentence I can practice consciousness-based healing," I said.

"Did the Being of Light tell you that?" she asked.

"Yes," I said.

"What did it sound like?" she asked.

"I'm not sure. It could have been a male voice or a female voice," I said. "I don't know how to explain it, because it was both things at the same time. In fact, it didn't talk to me out loud, and instead gave me information telepathically. It passed thoughts into my mind," I said.

Arpana looked at me skeptically.

"Telepathically," she repeated, shaking her head and smiling.

I knew we had a long way to go.

Chapter 12

The Open Road

In fairness to Arpana, she had never really heard of a near-death experience. Being a dentist, she had heard of people being overdosed with anesthesia or having cardiac arrests in the dental chair, but she had never heard of someone leaving his or her body, going into a tunnel, or visiting dead relatives in a heavenly realm. The idea of something like this happening was new to her, and the notion that it had happened to her husband was incomprehensible.

The subject of my NDE became the eight-hundred-pound gorilla in the hospital room. We didn't want to talk about it, but she could tell from the disconnected nature of our conversation that the experience was very much on my mind. She avoided the subject for a while but finally realized she had to break her silence on the subject.

"I'm sorry to act this way, Raja (her endearing name for me), but to me, it seems like a dream—a very vivid dream but a dream nonetheless," she said.

"But that's just it; it was not a dream. I was out of my body, I was there, and I received life-changing information," I said. "If it wasn't a real experience, do you think I would even entertain making such huge changes in our life?"

"These *are* huge changes, my Raja (my prince)," she said, using her endearing nickname for me. "But I can't help but question them. Our entire lives will change completely. Can we survive change like that?"

I understood exactly what she meant. If I quit my job as chief of anesthesiology, our friends would think I was critically ill and perhaps dying. If we sold our house and got rid of our expensive cars, they would think we were broke or possibly even divorcing. If I began talking about angels and consciousness-based healing, they would think I had gone crazy. She was right to question the moves I wanted to make. In our world—in almost any world—massive changes like the ones I was being asked to make would be the sign of a dire situation, not a spiritual change. Spiritual change would be the last thing most people would think of and the thing they would most likely disbelieve if it were offered as an explanation. Plus, I was being asked to make these changes by angels and a Being of Light that I met in the spirit world. *Am I crazy?* I thought.

"I don't know if we can survive such a change," I said, fearful at the notion of such a thing. "But I have to do what the angels and the Being of Light told me to do. They weren't asking. They talked about it as though change was a done deal!"

"So they saw our future," said Arpana, somewhat sarcastically.

"I guess so," I said. "They know what we have to do to fulfill my destiny."

I could hardly believe I was saying such a thing. I had always firmly believed I was in control of my life. For better or worse, I was the person who steered my destiny—our destiny. And now, giving up control to an angel must have seemed like total madness to anyone but me. Yet here I was, gladly giving up control of our lives in exchange for the promise of spiritual enlightenment.

"I have to take a walk," said Arpana.

"I have to take some painkiller," I responded, feeling the nerves around the open incision flare up.

I pressed the call button for the nurse. Before she arrived, Arpana was gone.

———

The next day the surgeon came to see how I was doing. My surgical incision was still open, but it was not oozing the way it had been the day before. In fact, the surgeon said it was healing very rapidly. "Remarkable progress," he said, poking at the incision with a gloved hand. "I think you're going to be out of here today."

Later in the afternoon, a resident came by to look at the incision. He poked and prodded until I squirmed. "Sorry, Doc," he said, "but if it didn't hurt, it wouldn't be healing."

He made a few notes in my file and told us that I would be leaving in the next few hours.

"Let's get you out of here before you catch a staph infection," he said, talking frankly to a colleague (me) about this serious contagion that plagues so many hospitals.

Within a few hours, discharge papers were signed, and I was wheeled out to the curb in a wheelchair to Arpana's BMW convertible. Before long, I was reclining in the passenger seat, and we were headed home.

We had driven this road many times, yet now I felt as though I was headed into a great unknown.

I had been prescribed a bottle of pain pills by the resident to get me through the two-hour ride home. He said that I was "pretty much tranquilized up" already, but if I needed more pain relief, the pills in the bottle should do the trick.

Ordinarily I would have welcomed the extra supply, because my dependency on pain pills mandated that I take them several times a day to avoid becoming depressed or angry. To my surprise, I put them in the glove box and didn't think of them again the entire trip.

My incision, which had been painful even with pain medication, was feeling much better than I thought it should. I even touched it a few times to make it hurt, just to make sure gangrene hadn't set in or there was some other unforeseen monster that might leave the area numb while it kills tissue. The pain wasn't great.

Something is changing, I told myself.

I could have said the same thing about Arpana. Yesterday she had been clearly upset about the change in me that had taken place, but now her face seemed relaxed and almost meditative. She wasn't smiling, but she seemed happy.

Once we got out of the congested traffic of Los Angeles and on the open road, Arpana began talking about the change coming in our future.

"It's like those rain clouds," she said, pointing to a bank of dark and threatening clouds on the horizon. "It is obviously going to rain sometime today but I can't tell if it is going to be a really bad thunderstorm or just a pleasant rain. I don't have enough information to know how bad the change will be or if it will be bad at all."

"I know what you mean," I said. "But it's easier for me because I was there and I know how real everything was. For you, it must be like hearing about a dream."

"A dream," said Arpana. "It's like basing our future on a dream."

Dream. I looked out the window and mulled that word in my mind: *dream.* My head dropped to my chest and I fell asleep. In a moment, I was dreaming. But rather than dreaming of more toys, as I often did, or dreaming of endlessly running across the desert, as I frequently did when falling asleep in front of the television set, I dreamed of starting a medical office dedicated to consciousness-based healing. I could see it perfectly. In my dream I was confused, not truly knowing what I was doing, only that I was doing something. Then suddenly I woke up.

Arpana was speaking.

"How can you make a career out of consciousness-based healing?" she asked. "What is it anyway?"

"I don't really know, not fully," I said. "It is how nonpharmacological treatments in combination with drugs can heal things like depression and addiction and other diseases. It's about searching one's own soul to fight back against the hollowness that pharmaceuticals alone or alcohol and illegal drugs create or don't really fill. You know what they say: *Addiction can be the result of an unfulfilled spiritual journey.*"

"Who says that?" Arpana asked.

I took a deep breath and answered: "The angels."

"But, Raja, you might have problems of your own," she said, looking at me with the full knowledge that I *indeed did* have problems of my own. "How can *you* teach those healing principles to someone else?"

My face flushed with shame. I knew what Arpana was talking about. When I didn't have enough pain medication to appease my dependency, I was easily angered and difficult to be around.

"I know I've had drug problems, but this is the time to cure it and teach others the secrets of that cure," I said. "I know this is the time to be taught this. I have a lot to learn about consciousness-based healing, but they said I will learn it. I have to believe."

I dozed off for a few miles and was awakened again by Arpana, who was shaking me by my shoulder.

"I've just been thinking," she said, a slight glint in her eyes. "I never wanted all of the stuff. You are the one who wanted it."

"What do you mean?" I asked, shaking my head to wake up.

"You wanted it all. You wanted the bigger house, the Hummer, the Mercedes, the parties, all the other toys."

Before I could defend myself, she told me about my desire to "hit the bull's-eye." I knew what she meant immediately. The development where our house was located was made up of two rings of houses. The outer ring consisted of upscale homes, ones that were 4,000 to 4,500 square feet, two stories, two-car garages, and a backyard and pool big enough to accommodate a party of thirty to forty guests comfortably. The second ring was the same as the outer except the houses were more than a thousand square feet bigger, the garage one car larger, and the backyard a party giver's delight. Oh, and to get to the second ring, one had to have a gate code. The second ring was the bull's-eye. The houses rivaled many in Beverly Hills for size and design. A small house in that ring was approximately 6,000 square feet, and the largest one, the scaled-down model of the White House, was about 11,000 square feet. The one we were living in had a lake and golf-course view, a garage for four cars, and hallway after hallway leading to room after room. The backyard had a pool, a hot tub, a fountain, and enough grass to keep a landscaper busy for half a day each week.

"Oh, the bull's-eye," I said. "How was I to know that was the beginning of my problems, not the end?"

"How were you to know? You should have thought about it," she said, pretending to be angry. "Now look at us! It's harder to get out of this position than into it."

But wait a minute, I thought. *I did not make these decisions alone.*

"Arpana, I wasn't the only one who bought these things. You were right there with me," I said. "You wanted them as much as I did."

Arpana sighed. "I know, Raja, I know. But the problem is that we all want more than we can afford. We are human. We don't know when to stop."

Chapter 13

True Healing

My eyes popped open as a faint glow came through the bedroom; the sun was just edging up over the horizon. Something had awakened me. *Was it a noise downstairs? Had I heard voices?*

I slowly and painfully turned over and faced Arpana. Her eyes were open, and she seemed wide awake. Her face looked as young as the day I met her more than twenty years earlier.

"I was talking to you. Sorry to wake you up," she said. "I've been thinking about what happened, and I think we should let events decide our course. How this unfolds will determine if it's real."

I was groggy. "What do you mean?" I asked.

"If what happened to you is just a dream, then nothing will happen. But if it was divine, then the angels will show themselves again, and we will follow them."

"What a wise wife I have," I said. "We should see what their guidance is and follow it."

"And if they give us guidance, I will believe that what you experienced was not a dream but reality," said Arpana.

"I am a lucky man," I said.

I could tell that she wasn't convinced that a near-death experience had taken place, but she was willing to see if the angels I spoke of would live up to their word. If that were the case and things began to happen in unexplained ways, then that would be proof a supernatural event had taken place.

I realized during the first few days after my surgery that Arpana was not relying totally on me for information about near-death experiences. She was cruising the Internet for information about what had happened. In her search she discovered the Near Death Experience Research Foundation, an excellent organization founded by Jeff Long, MD, and Jody Long, a husband-and-wife team with a passion for the study of NDEs. Their site contains more than thirty-five hundred near-death-experience case studies from all over the world, which gave her an opportunity to study this experience from the point of view of patients. By scanning these case studies, she found many similarities between my NDE and those of others.

She also purchased books by Raymond Moody, MD, PhD, the researcher whose work in the 1970s created the field of near-death studies and gave name to the "near-death experience."

His autobiography, *Paranormal: My Life in Pursuit of the Afterlife*, told the story of the research that defined and named the near-death experience. One of the most interesting portions of the book was the dissection of NDE case studies and the common traits among them that he discovered. By studying the elements that make up the NDE, Arpana was able to understand what I had gone through and perhaps what was in store.

These are the elements, set out in *Paranormal*, Moody found that define the near-death experience:

1. *Ineffability*: These experiences are virtually ineffable, or "inexpressible," because there are no words in our community of language to express consciousness at the point of death. That is why many people who've had NDEs say things like, "There are just no words to express what I am trying to say." This, of course, presents a problem because if one can't describe what's happened, they can't gain understanding from another person.

2. *Hearing the news*: Numerous people in the course of my research told of hearing their doctors or others pronounce them dead.

3. *Feelings of peace and quiet*: Many people described pleasant feelings and sensations during their experience, even after being pronounced dead. One man with a severe head injury and no detectable vital signs said that all pain vanished as he floated in a dark space and realized, "I must be dead."

4. *The noise*: In many of the cases, people reported unusual auditory sensations, like a loud buzzing noise or a loud ring. Some found this noise to be quite pleasant while others found it to be extremely annoying.

5. *The dark tunnel*: People reported the sensation of being pulled very rapidly through a dark space, most often described as being a tunnel. For instance, in one case a man who "died" several times during burns and fall injuries said that he escaped into a "dark void" in which he floated and tumbled through space.

6. *Out of the body*: During these experiences, usually after the tunnel experience, the people would have the sense of leaving their body and looking at themselves from a physical point outside of it. Some described it as being "the third person in the room," or like being "on a stage in a play." The experiences they had out of body were quite detailed and often involved an understanding that they were dead yet were observing their physical body. Many of the people described medical procedures and activity with such detail that there was little doubt on the part of attending physicians interviewed later that some kind of actual witnessing of events on the part of the comatose patient had occurred.

7. *Meeting others*: An out-of-body experience usually followed a tunnel experience, which was usually followed by the meeting of other "spiritual beings" in their vicinity, beings who were there to ease them through their transition and into death, or to tell them that it wasn't their time to die.

8. *The Being of Light*: The most incredible common element that I found and the one that had the greatest effect on the individual is the encounter with a very bright light, one that is most often described as a "Being of Light." This Being first appeared as a dim light and then became rapidly brighter until it reached an unearthly brilliance. Often described as "Jesus," "God," or an "angel" by those with religious training, the Light communicates with the individual (sometimes in a language they have never heard), often asking them if they are "ready to die," or what their accomplishments are.

The Being of Light does not ask these questions in a judgmental way. Rather it asks Socratic questions, ones aimed at acquiring information that can help the person proceed along a path of truth and self-realization.

The Being of Light or (just) Light is described as "unimaginable" or "indescribable" as well as "funny," "pleasant," or "secure."

9. *The review*: The probing questions of the Being of Light would often lead to a review of one's life, a moment of startling power during which a person's entire life was displayed before them in panoramic intensity. The review is extraordinarily rapid and in chronological order, and is incredibly vivid and real. Sometimes it is even described as "three-dimensional." Others describe it as "highly charged" with emotions and even multidimensional in a way that the individual can understand the thoughts of everyone in the review.

The review is most often described as an educational effort on the part of the Being of Light, one aimed at individuals understanding themselves better.

10. *The border or limit*: In some of these cases, the person describes approaching a "border" or "limit," beyond which they will not return. This border is described variously as being water, a gray mist, a door, a fence across a field, or even a line or an imaginary line.

In one such case, a person was escorted to the line by the Being of Light and asked if he wanted to die. When he said he knew nothing about death, the Being told him, "Come over this line and you will learn." When he did, he experienced "the most wonderful feeling" of peace, tranquility, and a vanishing of all worries.

11. *Coming back*: Obviously, the individuals I spoke with came back to their physical lives. Some resisted their return and wanted to stay in this afterlife state. Some reported return trips through the tunnel and back to their physical bodies. But when they did return, they had moods and feelings that lingered for a long time. Many were transformed and reported becoming "better" people.

12. *Telling others*: The people I spoke to were normal people with functioning, well-balanced personalities. Yet because they were afraid of being labeled as delusional or mentally ill, these people often chose to remain silent about their experience or only relate it to someone very close to them. Because there was no common language in which to express their experience, they chose to keep it to themselves so no one would think they had become mentally unbalanced as a result of their brush with death.

It wasn't until many individuals heard of the research I was doing that they felt comfortable enough to relate their experience to others. I was frequently thanked by these long-silent NDErs, who would say, "Thank you for your work. Now I know I'm not crazy."

13. *Effects on lives*: Despite the desire of most of these individuals to remain quiet about their experience, the effect of these experiences on their lives was profound and noticeable. Many told me their lives had broadened and deepened through these experiences, that they had become

more reflective of life and more gentle with those around them. Their vision left them with new goals, new moral principles, and a renewed determination to live in accordance with them.

14. *New views of death*: In the end they all reported new views about death. They no longer feared death yet many had the sense that they had a lot of personal growth to attend to before leaving their physical life. They also came to believe that there is no "reward and punishment" model of the afterlife. Rather, the Being of Light made their sinful deeds obvious to them and made it clear that life was a learning process, not a platform for later judgment.

Moody named these elements a "near-death experience" because a person who has them is not truly dead but close to death, sometimes as close to death as possible. He also pointed out that few, if any, of the people in his case studies had experienced all of these elements. Sometimes they experienced one or two and other times nearly all of them. Usually, he said, those who get closer to death experience more of the traits.

Moody went further with his NDE definition, describing a near-death episode as one in which a person is clinically dead, near death, or in a situation where death is likely. In all of these cases, a person is technically *not* dead but near death—hence the name, "near-death experience."

Moody's book was a quick read and gave Arpana the philosophical and medical underpinning to understand the seemingly supernatural events that had swept into our lives. By reading Moody's book, she realized it was rare for someone to have such a profound NDE as the one I had. Moody wrote that he rarely saw an NDE in which all of the traits he outlined were present. Yet Arpana could see that I had experienced all of them during my NDE and as a result was in the midst of a powerful transformation. She said later that reading Moody's book gave her help in understanding the phenomenon of NDEs but also caused her to fear it because Moody said he rarely encountered an individual who'd had all the traits of an NDE I had.

As she put it, "Being a rare patient means they don't know much about the extent of your case and you become an experiment."

I agreed with her assessment. Frankly, I felt like an experimental patient already.

I had been home from the hospital for three days.

When I wasn't sleeping, we were in constant conversation about materialism and how to live with less. I have to admit I was obsessing about materialism because overcoming this demon was the first change in my life the angels told me to make. I knew I had to do it to show them I was taking them seriously.

Sometimes my conversations with Arpana became tense as we compared our spending habits, blaming the other for the financial hole we had dug for ourselves. But for the most part, I knew the truth: I was the needy one in our family, the one who had to show his wealth to the world.

That night, before going to bed, I confessed to Arpana that I had entrapped our family in a world of materialism. "I am the problem, I know that," I said. "I am the one who was told by the Being of Light I must change."

"Okay," said Arpana. "If they give us good guidance, I will believe that what you experienced was not a dream but a reality."

I was thankful for her trust in my experience.

I closed my eyes, but sleep didn't come. Instead came a flood of memories, memories of my first meeting with Arpana.

Ours was an arranged marriage. In the Indian culture, it is traditional for the parents to come together with their friends and pair up their children for marriage.

I had moved from New Delhi to New York City and completed my US medical board tests as well as a medical residency in pediatrics when my father announced that he was ready for me to meet with the fathers of several eligible daughters.

I agreed to return to India for this traditional yet nerve-wracking process. I had told my father that I would accept this tradition only on the condition that I be allowed to select a woman I liked and that she in turn liked me. Before he started his search for my potential partner, I insisted on three things: that she be beautiful, smart, and interested in having her own career.

When I arrived in India, he had fifteen women ready for me, their nervous fathers in tow.

After a week of constant meetings, I hadn't found a single woman I liked.

My father tried to cover for his finicky son and not embarrass the fathers at the same time. He told each of their unhappy fathers that I liked their daughters very much but an astrologer had rejected each one on the grounds of a poor astrological match.

"They may become angry with me if I say you did not want to be married to their daughter," my father told me. "But no one will argue with the universe."

A few months later, I returned to India to face another dozen women who had been arranged by my persevering father. The fifth woman I met was Arpana. I met with her for a half hour and we fell in love. We were everything the other one wanted: medical professionals with a desire for family, a good sense of humor, and serious about getting ahead economically. We decided to marry.

Since I had only two weeks of vacation from my hospital, we had to marry quickly. I saw her for the first time on January 29, we became engaged two days later, and we were married on February 12. In America, that time schedule might be considered a shotgun wedding. In India, it was considered turning one's life over to the universe.

I returned to the United States, leaving Arpana in India waiting for a visa. My mother called, making her needs known.

"I want to be a grandmother soon," she demanded.

"Mom," I said, "I plan to work very hard at it."

Eight months later, Arpana came to the United States, and within one month she was pregnant with our first child.

My career had us moving all over the country. We went to Nashville, then to Shreveport, Louisiana, where I was a resident in anesthesiology at Louisiana State University hospital. Then we got an opportunity to go to Bakersfield, California, for two weeks of work at San Joaquin Community Hospital. I took a liking to California with its warm weather and open thought. When the hospital offered me a staff position, I accepted it immediately and stayed there for several years until I was offered one of the most challenging positions an anesthesiologist can have: cardiac anesthesiologist at a major heart hospital. My job would be to provide anesthesiology services to high-risk heart patients. Eventually I became the chief of anesthesiology.

In many ways, I had reached the top of my profession; I had achieved all of my goals and then some. Arpana too had achieved her goals. We had three children—a girl and two boys—and Arpana somehow found time to complete the California State dental examinations and open a successful practice.

Why hadn't I been happy with our high achievement? I asked myself. *Why did I have to be materialistic to prove I was somebody?*

I remembered a famous quote that had always been a puzzle to me: One never knows what is enough until they know what is too much. Now, as I lay in bed in the early morning with Arpana next to me, I finally knew exactly what it meant.

I knew my true healing was about to begin.

Chapter 14

Transformed by the Light

I had been home only a few days when we were visited by one of our friends, a plastic surgeon living in the first ring of the bull's-eye. He listened in stunned silence as I recounted my experience, enthralled with what he heard and nodding his head like a child listening to a thrilling adventure story.

"You remind me of Scrooge," he said, referring to the lead character in Charles Dickens's *A Christmas Carol*, in which three ghosts show him his past, present, and future in disturbing detail. Many literary experts consider the events of this story to be a near-death experience, and it might well have been, given that Ebenezer Scrooge was transformed by his life review. He went from being a materialistic grouch to a man of great humor and generosity, all in one night of encounters with three supernatural beings.

Arpana laughed when she heard that comparison; in fact, we all did, even me. Being compared to Scrooge after my NDE meant I was the good Scrooge, the one who had been transformed by the Being of Light, not the one who lived in the darkness of remorse, materialism, and paranoia.

But transformation doesn't come easily. I am sure Scrooge had difficulty. I know I did. Although much of my new life depended on eliminating materialism, I wasn't certain how to do it. We'd had serious talks about putting our house on the market, but neither of us reached for the telephone to call a realtor. There was something about having a "for sale" sign in our front yard that seemed like an irretrievable loss of status.

"What will the neighbors think if we do this?" asked Arpana.

We were sitting in the backyard having afternoon tea when she posed the question. The yellow light of the setting sun skimmed the deep green grass and made the colorfully dressed golfers look like subjects in a living painting. It was a perfect day.

"They'll think we are crazy or broke," I said.

Somehow we thought the neighbors really cared. We thought they would talk behind our backs if we told them we planned to move into more affordable housing. After all, coupled with a downgrade of vehicles in our driveway, we were sure to become the talk of the bull's-eye, weren't we? Neither of us wanted that kind of humiliation, and we sat worrying about our image in the community while we sipped our tea against that stunning backdrop of the man-made nature that was the golf course.

For a moment, I hate to admit, I even began to question the true message of the angels.

The next day the plastic surgeon returned, this time with his girlfriend. He made an unexpected proposal.

"Let's swap houses," he said.

Within an hour we agreed to the particulars of a trade. We lost more money than I want to admit, but by the end of the day, we had a house payment that was less than a quarter of the house we currently lived in and, yes, a home that was half the size of ours. Without anyone in the neighborhood knowing, we had just sold our house.

"As soon as I get well, we'll start moving," I said to the surgeon.

"Take your time, and don't do anything that will make you feel worse," he said. "I'll pretend I'm not in a hurry."

I appreciated his concern for my healing. My surgery had consisted of five surgical wounds so pus could be sucked out of my abdominal cavity with a device that looks like a turkey baster, and then swabbed out of my abdominal cavity in the same way that a dishwasher would scrub a pan clean. Yet within seventy-two hours, I was discharged home. Now, less than two weeks after the surgery, I started to examine my near-death experience. Would I let it change my life?

I had become an experiment of one—my own first study patient in researching the mysteries of consciousness-based healing. In short, I was a guinea pig in the exploration of disease of the soul. Whatever healing power the Being of Light had left me was working with great effect on me. Still, my surgical wounds were sometimes painful, leaving me tired and spiritually concerned for my future well-being, but still I was healing rapidly. It was now my goal to find out how to be a conduit for this universal healing energy and to help the suffering of others.

———

Over the next few days, I read more about near-death experiences from multiple sources, especially individuals who had been healed and developed healing power from a Being of Light or some other mystical light source like I had. I also searched for others who had had experiences of Light.

These Lights or Beings of Light have been described in a variety of ways by those who had experienced an NDE. One said they are like human beings "only without the overcoat" or "angels of the higher plane." Others say they appear as "dazzling lights" so bright they cannot be looked at. In almost all cases, they report that these mystical Lights or Beings of Light leave them with something: words of wisdom, or a higher goal for them to achieve, or a serenity that they have never before had, or knowledge or new direction, or even a newfound sense of humor. The list of possible spiritual treasures from this mystical light source goes on and on.

It is these encounters with the mystical Light or Beings of Light that have been shown in medical studies to be the most transformative aspect of the near-death experience. For example a survey of case studies compiled by the International Association of Near Death Studies (IANDS) done by Nancy Evans Bush found several in which encounters with the mystical Light seemed to equate to being born into a spiritual realm. One short case study that illustrates this point came from a thirty-nine-year-old graphic artist who had suffered a cardiac arrest at the age of five after being electrocuted: "I found myself falling down a tunnel with colored ridges that led down to a bright Light. I fell slowly at first and then began to fall faster and faster. The faster I went, the better I felt. I wanted to reach the Light but I couldn't. Even though I never reached the Light, I think it has changed the way I feel about life and death. It has certainly made me feel more spiritual and loving."

In another case study in the IANDS archive, a fourteen-year-old boy was swept from a bridge by raging floodwaters. He was rescued and wrote about the incident years later:

I knew I was either dead or going to die. But then something happened. It was so immense, so powerful, that I gave up on my life to see what it was. I wanted to venture into this experience, which started as drifting into what I could only describe as a long, rectangular tunnel of Light. But it wasn't just Light, it was a protective passage of energy with an intense brightness at the end which I wanted to look into, to touch.

. . . As I reached the source of the Light, I could see in. I cannot begin to describe in human terms the feelings I had over what I saw. It was a giant infinite world of calm, and love, and energy, and beauty. . . . It was all being, all beauty, all meaning for all existence. It was all the energy of the Universe forever in one place.

As I reached my right hand into it, feelings of exhilarating anticipation overwhelmed me. I did not need my body anymore. I wanted to leave it behind and go to my God in this new world.

With so many who have experiences of Light, the world of this young man made more sense, and things fit together more coherently. And most important, life seemed to have greater purpose.

Melvin Morse, MD, in *Closer to the Light*, his classic book on children and near-death experiences, describes the mystical Light as a driving force for spirituality in an individual. As anecdotal proof, he refers to many spiritual leaders who have had an experience of Light that changed their life and direction.

One of those was the Indian guru Paramahansa Yogananda, who in *Autobiography of a Yogi* describes his near-death experience at age eight, which then enhanced his lifelong devotion to religion. He wrote: "There [was] a blinding Light, enveloping my body and the entire room. My nausea and other uncontrollable symptoms disappeared; I was well." This Light stayed with Yogananda the rest of his life. Not only was he able to be exposed to the Light when he meditated, he was also able to call on it to illuminate others. This ability of "revisiting the Light," as I came to call it, was something I soon realized I was able to do too, which led to further life changes.

Jonathan Edwards, the eighteenth-century Calvinist theologian, had a lot to say about the Light at the end of the tunnel. In his childhood, he nearly died of pneumonia. Later, as a preacher in New York and New England, Edwards wrote from experience of the "spiritual and divine Light": "There is such a thing as a spiritual and divine Light, immediately imparted to the soul by God, of a different nature from any obtained by natural means." The Light, he wrote, can be described as "a spiritual and saving conviction of the truth and reality of divine glory. It is sweet and pleasant to the soul . . . [and allows us] to see the mutual relations between things and occasions us to take more notice of them."

What exactly is the divine Light, and where does it reside? Morse did not say; rather he declares that these experiences of Light have a religious quality to them, one that allows people to experience a divine world that seems to exist on a different plane from the physical one we occupy. As he wrote: "It has long been my belief that many of the world's great religious leaders have been driven by profound near-death and other visionary experiences that involve the mystical Light. There are many such examples—both great and small—of people being turned toward a life of devotion by the Light."

One such person was Bill Wilson, perhaps one of the great healers in modern history, who devised what may be the most effective means of spiritual healing after having an NDE.

Wilson, also known as "Bill W.," was the cofounder of Alcoholics Anonymous, the worldwide organization that uses a series of spiritual guidelines known as the twelve steps to defeat addiction.

Wilson was the primary author of the book *Alcoholics Anonymous*, which has been the healing guide for millions of alcoholics and drug addicts since it was written in 1938.

Wilson developed this spiritual program for recovery after his own encounter with a Being of Light in 1934. In that year, he had committed himself to a clinic aimed at curing alcohol addiction. He had gone to the clinic to keep from drinking himself to death and was treated with a dose of belladonna, a plant used frequently as a treatment for alcoholism.

It was after that treatment that Dr. William Silkworth, the clinic's director, asked Wilson if he would like to dedicate himself to Jesus to see if such an act would rid him of his alcoholism. Depressed and filled with despair, Wilson began to weep. "I'll do anything! Anything at all! If there be a God, let him show himself!" he shouted.

Bill described the experience in this way:

The effect was instant, electric. Suddenly my room blazed with an incredibly white Light. I was seized with an ecstasy beyond description. I have no words for this.

Every joy I had known was pale by comparison.

The Light, the ecstasy. I was conscious of nothing else for a time.

Then, seen in the mind's eye, there was a mountain. I stood upon its summit where a great wind blew. A wind, not of air, but of spirit. In great, clean strength it blew right through me. Then came the blazing thought, "You are a free man." I know not at all how long I remained in this state, but finally the Light and the ecstasy subsided. . . . As I became more quiet a great peace stole over me, and this was accompanied by a sensation difficult to describe. I became acutely conscious of a presence which seemed like a veritable sea of living spirit. I lay on the shores of a new world. "This," I thought, "must be the great reality. The God of the preachers."

Later, when he told Dr. Silkworth what had happened, the doctor was perplexed but happy, describing the event as "some great psychic occurrence, something that I don't understand. I've read of these things in books, but I've never seen one before. You have had some kind of conversion experience. . . . You are already a different individual. Something has happened to you I don't understand. But you had better hang on to it."

Wilson hung on to it the rest of his life and never drank again. He told Dr. Bob Smith, an alcoholic in Akron, Ohio, about his experience, and the doctor began to pursue a "spiritual remedy" for his own alcoholism. Except for a brief relapse, Dr. Smith never drank again either. The two men, Bill W. and Dr. Bob, became the founders of Alcoholics Anonymous.

Throughout his life, Bill Wilson insisted he was just an ordinary man. Few agreed with that assessment. Biographer Susan Cheever, in her biography of Wilson, *My Name Is Bill*, wrote of the AA founder as a synthesizer of ideas, the man who pulled together various threads of psychology, theology, and democracy into a workable and lifesaving system. Author Aldous Huxley was quoted in *Time* magazine as calling Wilson "the greatest social architect of our century"; *Time* magazine also said he was a "healer" and named him to its 1993 list of the 100 most important people of the twentieth century. Wilson was more modest. He called himself a man who, "because of his bitter experience, discovered, slowly and through a conversion experience, a system of behavior and a series of actions that work for alcoholics who want to stop drinking."

The twelve steps developed for Alcoholics Anonymous are

a masterful piece of spiritual guidance. Whether one believes in NDEs, spiritual transformation, or even in God, the AA program takes all of that into consideration. An addict who participates in AA isn't asked to believe in any or all of the tenets of the twelve steps. Rather they are just asked to participate in them for a period of time during which many of the initiates will begin to feel the benefits of a spiritual approach to their problem, generally through a sponsor who is a veteran of the program.

The AA program, wrote French philosopher Michel Foucault in his work on liberation philosophy, noted that such practices as confession, penitence, meditation, and the writing of a moral inventory produce "intrinsic modifications in the person—exonerating, redeeming and purifying them; relieves them of their burden of wrong, liberating them and promising salvation."

It is easy to confuse AA with a religious organization, especially when looking at the program's twelve steps. Yet AA declares that the use of the word *spirituality* doesn't have the same meaning as the word *religious*. For many in AA, "spiritual" refers to living the reality of life and being in touch with one's own feelings, "character defects," and "gifts."

It is through this spiritual awakening that one might come into touch with God. Or not. The goal of the twelve-step program is not religious. Rather, it is a process in which one learns to stop drinking and drugging, and through that may experience the higher power of what many of us call God.

The original twelve steps are:

1. We admitted we were powerless over alcohol—that our lives had become unmanageable.
2. Came to believe that a Power greater than ourselves could restore us to sanity.

3. Made a decision to turn our will and our lives over to the care of God *as we understood Him*.

4. Made a searching and fearless moral inventory of ourselves.

5. Admitted to God, to ourselves, and to another human being the exact nature of our wrongs.

6. Were entirely ready to have God remove all these defects of character.

7. Humbly asked Him to remove our shortcomings.

8. Made a list of all persons we had harmed, and became willing to make amends to them all.

9. Made direct amends to such people wherever possible, except when to do so would injure them or others.

10. Continued to take personal inventory and when we were wrong promptly admitted it.

11. Sought through prayer and meditation to improve our conscious contact with God *as we understood Him*, praying only for knowledge of His will for us and the power to carry that out.

12. Having had a spiritual awakening as the result of these steps, we try to carry this message to alcoholics and to practice these principles in all our affairs.

When I look at the twelve steps, I can't help but think that Wilson's encounter with the Light was similar to my own with the Being of Light. I also couldn't help but think that he too was asked to devise a means of spiritual healing much like the one I was being asked to devise.

Although Wilson didn't report having a conversation with the Light, it appears obvious that he received some kind of information during his experience that allowed him to compile the twelve steps and create one of the great international institutions of healing. His encounter with the Light also stopped his addiction cold and resulted in an important self-realization: "I had to be the first in everything because in my perverse heart I felt myself to be the least of God's creatures."

My encounter with the Light had done something similar to me, and to be honest, it was somewhat frightening. Following my surgery, I realized my addiction to painkillers was rapidly abating. This was no small thing. Pain pills and antidepressants had almost taken over my life.

An addiction psychiatrist I once consulted with told me that stopping any "grave dependency" would take weeks in rehab to overcome. For months, I wondered how I could recover from addiction and keep my job. After all, a slight medical error on my part could have grave consequences in the operating room. But now I was no longer craving more pills than were prescribed. My appetite for a drug high disappeared quickly. Prescribed pain pill doses were sufficient and sometimes not even necessary. Soon I took less than what was prescribed and only as needed for my pelvic pain. I longed to do the same thing with the antidepressants. I was sure that the Being of Light was healing me as it had others who had experienced the same spiritual transformation.

I wanted to be free!

Chapter 15

Lucky Rajiv or Poor Rajiv

There are two basic types of psychiatrist: the ones who talk to you and the ones who don't.

The ones who practice the "talking cure" are the ones who don't rely totally on pharmaceuticals and believe that well-worded questions and a genuine interest in patients can provide healing solutions to problems that plague the human mind. This would be especially true of a doctor like C. G. Jung, for instance, the father of analytical psychology, who had an NDE himself. After his experience, he could speak in talk therapy at a personal level of understanding so deep that people who have had an NDE would know he or she had the right doctor when the doctor said something like: "What happens after death is so unspeakably glorious that our imagination and feelings do not suffice to form even an approximate conception of it."

Then there are the doctors who don't talk. They ask a few questions, then prescribe meds, usually something for depression or sleeping.

Most patients want to see the doctor who doesn't talk.

Yes, even in this self-obsessed age where we love to log in to a variety of Internet sites and talk endlessly about ourselves and our deepest personal feelings to total strangers, there are relatively few people who express a preference for talk over drug therapy. The reason is that most people prefer a pharmaceutical solution. Because of that and the advent of managed care, only about 10 percent of psychiatrists spend more than fifteen minutes with their patients in an appointment.

I too was that kind of doctor. If a patient was willing to summarize his or her complaint, I, like many other doctors, would write a prescription and send the patient on their way in less time than the average coffee break.

If the first prescription doesn't work, many doctors are willing to provide a second to make the first more effective. And if the first two drugs result in side effects, it might be possible to lessen those side effects with a third miracle pill. If pills don't work, then the same physician might refer the patient to a psychologist to talk, or a psychiatrist for more medication. It is the antithesis of consciousness-based healing as I am now learning to practice it, but it's also a typical approach to both addiction and pain, physical and psychological, in the Western world.

Sadly, even when addicted patients want to find other coping mechanisms in order to reduce their pill intake, the relapse rate for those taking pain pills and antidepressants is extremely high. Just reducing dependence below the threshold for addiction, as I did, is often compared to stopping cold turkey. And this is where lengthy and expensive rehab visits or a doctor's guidance are vital. Without the proper medical guidance, a patient may run the risk of severe withdrawal symptoms, including seizures or hallucinations.

Amazingly, none of that happened to me over the months it took me to reduce my dependence on pain pills and mood-altering medications. Perhaps my medical knowledge made the difference; I don't know. What I do know is that after my NDE, I eventually walked out of my old life and into a world where addiction didn't exist.

I don't mean to imply that the changes in my life occurred without effort, but that my encounter with the angels and the Being of Light gave me the knowledge and insight I needed to make the effort to transform my life.

There was much to transform. Before my NDE, I had suffered from serious wrist pain that required surgery, then long-term depression, which worsened once I was diagnosed with prostate cancer. Looming large among my real-life problems was the money I had lost in the stock market—more than $3.5 million, much of it belonging to other members of my family. There were existential questions as well. Why did I get cancer? Why did the complications increase during the first six surgeries? Surgery usually makes addiction worse: I not only wanted pain pills, I needed them too. All this pain was so severe that I took disability on multiple occasions. Still, how could I have lost control over my treatment? How much longer could I work long hours in the intense world of high-risk heart surgeries? Was it right for me to operate a pain clinic when I had the same dependency issues as some of my patients? Why had I become so hopelessly materialistic and needlessly competitive? How could I mend my relationship with my son, my father, or my God?

After my NDE, I realized that my angels could lead me to the answers.

I felt compelled to meditate after returning home from the hospital, and now I was doing it daily, sometimes several times a day. I even took over a room on the first floor of our new house, a small den that I fitted with some statues of Hindu gods and goddesses and statues of St. Michael and St. Raphael, the Christian saints who had appeared to me. It was a strange mix of religions, made even stranger by the blue smoke that filled the room when I lit incense. Still, I liked the mix. One of the many things I was made to realize by my contact with the angels and the Being of Light was the sameness between people and religions. I was made to realize all of this through an encounter during meditation with Michael. "No matter what our religion preaches, the truth is that we all want the same thing," Michael had said, his voice filling my head just before he appeared. "We all want health, happiness, freedom from fear, and unity. We all just want to get along."

There were other encounters with the angels. In fact, they came to me often as I meditated, though I could not predict when they might appear. Sometimes they were just there. Other times they were like teachers in a classroom. If I was pondering a question during my meditation, for example, they often entered the picture to help answer it.

One day when I was meditating, a deep sadness came over me, caused by some of the same concerns that had driven me into depression. I began to think about the money I had lost in the stock market in 1999 and wondered why I had put all of my capital at risk just to try to make more when what I had already made was more than I ever expected. I thought about friends who had made many more times the amount I had lost by following my advice. Why hadn't I stopped trading stock options and cashed in at the same time I told them to? Then I began to wonder why I had gotten prostate cancer. Had God given it to me? And why had I continued to get sick and require so many surgeries? Was this karmic payback for something I had done? Was this going to stop? Would I ever feel good about myself again?

I struggled to stay in a positive meditative state, which generally means letting the thoughts come and go, accepting them as being a part of life, and letting them disappear into the mental cosmos. But they would not disappear. They stayed with me and threatened to ruin my meditation session.

Then both Michael and Raphael appeared. In their pleasant way, they calmed me down, telling me that "going off the track" during meditation was common.

"When you meditate, you are supposed to let thoughts arise, but detach from them, let them float downstream in the river of life," said Raphael.

"Yes, that's what's supposed to happen," agreed Michael. "But that doesn't happen to most people, at least not in the beginning."

"Yes, thoughts have thorns, just like cactus," said Raphael. "They stick to you and they hurt. Sometimes they don't detach as quickly as you would like, and they hurt even when they do."

There were easy ways to conquer these depressing thoughts, said Michael. It was all a matter of changing perspective. To do that, Michael recommended I develop two opposing personalities, Poor Rajiv and Lucky Rajiv. Poor Rajiv is the man who is stressed out because he lost money in the stock market and can't accept that the losses were caused by his greed. Then he got cancer, and with it came multiple surgeries with complications. Now he blames God for his problems instead of considering his own karma. Lucky Rajiv is that guy who has a chance to follow his dharma, his purpose, and doesn't have a huge mortgage. His life is easier, and he can explore a new meaning of life, maybe even change the world.

These two versions of me were to become my new frame of

reference. The angels told me to ponder the question during meditation: *Which one do I want to be today? Lucky Rajiv or Poor Rajiv?*

I realized I could change the story around the circumstances of my life. As Raphael said, "You cannot prevent pain, but suffering is an option."

All I had to do was change the perspective, and I didn't have to suffer. It became just that simple. I couldn't change the past; I had to accept it. And with that I realized I could choose to be lucky or unfortunate. In other words, I can do nothing about the pain of the past, but I can stop suffering about it and make the future what I want.

Chapter 16

The Story He Had Not Heard

Of course I am not the first person in medicine to follow a spiritual path. There have been many others whose lives have been changed by mystical experiences. C. G. Jung, one of the fathers of psychotherapy, is perhaps the best-known person of medicine to take that spiritual fork in the road.

Jung was a student and good friend of Sigmund Freud. So close were the two that Freud often called Jung his "eldest son," and Jung called Freud "shrewd and altogether remarkable." But their mutual respect began to change in 1913, with an injury to the sixty-eight-year-old Jung that led to a heart attack while in the hospital. During the heart attack, Jung had what would come to be known as a near-death experience.

After the horror of feeling the intense pain in his chest and losing consciousness, Jung said he found himself floating a thousand miles above earth. He could see all, he declared: the deep blue seas, the beige Arabian desert, and the snow-tipped Himalayas.

As he circled the earth, a gigantic black temple appeared. At the doorway was a Hindu sitting in a lotus position. Finding millions of candles flickering, Jung had the uncomfortable feeling of having his earthly existence stripped away, leaving him with only the core of his experiences, which he called "the essential Jung."

He was certain that the temple held the purpose of his life and edged cautiously past the man in lotus position and toward the temple door so he could find his life's meaning. He didn't make it. As he approached the doorway, he saw the image of his own doctor rising from Europe far below in the form of an ancient physician, "King Kos," who resided in the temple of Asclepius, the Greek god of medicine. The doctor told Jung that it wasn't his time to die and that many on earth were demanding his return. When Jung resisted the return, the doctor told him that he had been sent to this heavenly realm to bring him back.

Several days after the near-death experience, Jung sat up in bed and told his story. His greatest concern of all, he told those around him, was that his personal doctor, the doctor who had been sent to bring him back, would now have to sacrifice his life. Jung did not say why such a sacrifice would have to take place, but a few days later, when the psychotherapist sat up in bed (April 4, 1944, or 4/4/44 for those with a numerological interest), Jung's doctor died of blood poisoning.

Jung's NDE led to a split with Sigmund Freud, who believed that spiritual experiences were fantasies. Jung, however, considered spirituality an important part of our well-being, saying that life has purpose beyond material goals and that our main task, the path we should all be on, is the one that leads to our own connection with the universe. He also split from Freud on religion. Where Freud viewed religion with an atheist's eye, calling it a "collective neurosis" caused by a "longing for father," Jung's studies of the great religions led him to believe that self-discovery and transformation are at the heart of all religions. Jung stated in *The Red Book*:

> The decisive question for man is: Is he related to something infinite or not? That is the telling question of his life. Only if we know that the thing which truly matters is the infinite can we avoid fixing our interest upon futilities, and upon all kinds of goals which are not of real importance. . . . The more a man lays stress on false possessions, and the less sensitivity he has for what is essential, the less satisfying is his life. . . . If we understand and feel that here in this life we already have a link with the infinite, desires and attitudes change. In the final analysis, we count for something only because of the essential we embody, and if we do not embody that, life is wasted.

The spiritual path Jung took after his near-death experience is not always easily understood. He denied a belief in God because he had come to know God. "Knowledge trumps belief," he said. "Once you come to know something, you no longer have to believe in it." He felt we live in a culture that strips all things of their mystery and presence of God so that "nothing is holy any longer." For Jung, religion was "the attitude peculiar to a consciousness which has been changed by experience of the *numinosum* (*spirit of God*)."

I didn't have to fully understand his spiritual philosophy or belief (or lack of it) in God. When it came to Jung, all I needed for inspiration were two quotes that I found in a book of his collected essays. One is about the role we play in who we are: "It is often tragic to see how blatantly a man bungles his own life and the lives of others yet remains totally incapable of seeing how much the whole tragedy originates in himself, and how he continually feeds it and keeps it going." The other is about the role of spirituality in medicine: "It must gradually be dawning on any responsible doctor what a tremendously important role the spiritual element plays in the psychic economy."

———

Many of my friends didn't understand why I was ready to leave my distinguished post as chief anesthesiologist.

One of the first colleagues to hear my experience was aghast at even the notion of a near-death experience. I hadn't seen him for some time when we attended a medical conference near San Francisco. He was glad to see me and asked how I was feeling after my surgery. I didn't intend to tell him about my NDE, but as I started telling him about the events leading up to the emergency surgery, I slipped over into the events of my NDE. He listened patiently as I told him the experience but came unglued when he heard that my father had rescued me from hell.

In his religion, he said, he had been taught that NDEs were the work of Satan and that anyone who believed in them was flirting with the devil.

"But I don't feel like this is the work of the devil," I said.

"I understand," he said. "And that is how the devil works. You can't tell if he's behind something like this because he deceives you."

The conversation left me speechless and embarrassed, not only for him but for me. I felt sorry for the man. There was no way that my NDE could be considered a work of the devil. If anything, it was God's harsh lesson in redemption. But an act of deception by an evil being? Certainly not.

Because of that encounter, I decided to keep quiet about my experience for a while and digest what had happened. Until I could fully understand the experience myself, I decided to be very selective to whom I told the story, even leaving it out of my writing about health and wellness.

———————

The next person I told about my NDE was my best friend, Naresh. We had not known each other in India but had met in Bakersfield over two decades before. It was our habit to often have lunch at an Italian restaurant where we would talk about family, work, and sports.

Over the last year our conversations had taken a sad turn. Naresh had been diagnosed with cancer and the doctors had found it late. He'd had surgery and chemotherapy, but it had metastasized to other parts of his body. Most recently his doctors had discovered lesions in his liver.

We both knew his condition was grave. He had stage 4 cancer, which meant his disease was now firmly present in many parts of his body. We spoke as positively as we could about his prognosis, but we both knew it was grim. Still, we did what most people do: we avoided the subject of mortality. Instead we discussed his disease in surface terms, rarely addressing the likely outcome of this horrible disease. Usually our meals would start with me asking how he felt, to which he would answer, "Fine." We then spent the rest of the meal trying to talk around this enormous subject. *If we ignore it, maybe it will go away*, we thought. *Or maybe we just won't feel the discomfort of talking about death.* But ignoring it proved impossible, and soon our meetings were sad affairs because we knew that he would not be alive much longer.

Finally one day Naresh came to the restaurant and announced that he was going to have an experimental surgery, one in which the surgeon would try to burn the lesion from the liver. Naresh knew that such a surgery would almost surely not work. Still, he said he had to try. "I have no choice," he said.

I agreed. Even knowing that the surgery would afford only a slim chance for recovery, I would try everything I could to stay alive, if not just for me, but for my family too. But I was also no longer frightened of death, and the reason was the events of my near-death experience and the fact that it offered good news about life after death.

I would be sorry to see my friend go, but I now knew that the death of our physical body was not the death of our consciousness. I didn't know where we go after our earthly life, not totally, but I knew from my experience that we were still somewhere in the cosmos, living a different and wholly beautiful existence.

At this point I hadn't told him about my experience. Since my opening up to my friend at the medical conference hadn't gone well, I had decided to keep the story to myself for a while longer. But now I realized Naresh had only a short time to live. I decided I could help him, if not with the comfort of my own spiritual experience, then at least with the humor it might bring at hearing a friend talk about an experience he might find completely ludicrous.

I remember the moment I told him. He was talking about his upcoming surgery and how the surgeon was going to cauterize his tumor. He knew the risk of this surgery, which included the possibility of uncontrolled bleeding. He was uncomfortable talking about it, and his voice cracked when he told me that he feared the operation. "There's nothing else I can do," he said, his hands fidgeting with the utensils next to his untouched plate of food. "There is nothing else left to do, and I'm frightened."

He spoke about his fears—those for his family and those for himself and how he believed his consciousness would be obliterated at the moment of his death. He expressed his concern about the shortness of life, the unfairness of disease, and he wondered what the future held for his wife and children.

"I don't want to die," he said. "But I fear I will soon have no choice."

"That may be true," I said, beginning slowly and awkwardly. "Life can seem cruel. But I have not yet told you what happened when I had my surgery. I had what is known as a near-death experience. I can tell you what happens at death."

Then I began telling him the part of the story he didn't know: what happened during my NDE.

I think Naresh was surprised. He had, of course, heard about my surgery, but not about the part that should have been occupied by the impenetrable darkness of anesthesia. So I told him the story. From the moment I told of leaving my body until I recounted the story of the anesthesiologist in recovery and the joke I should not have heard, Naresh was absorbed.

"You will be there for your family, but in spiritual form," I assured him.

With the telling of my story, the conversation between us changed. He admitted that he and his wife had begun to look at me as Poor Rajiv. He said they thought I had lost my nerve about my life and my work. He said they even thought my prostate cancer had returned.

Now, after I told him about my experience, he realized what had happened: I had taken another path. He now saw me as Lucky Rajiv, a person who had discovered his true calling in life, a person who was shown his true path in life and decided to take it.

After this day, our meetings took a turn for the better. We began to speak much more honestly about our feelings about the meaning of life and the mystery of death. And as we spoke more openly, the gulf between us narrowed. There were no longer subjects we had to avoid. By virtue of my freely discussing my mystical experience, a new world of friendship opened between us, one that was honest, brave, and ready to explore the possibilities of the spiritual universe.

I soon realized some truths about life after death: Not only does everyone think about it, but the conclusions they make have a profound effect on the path of life they choose from then on. As a result of his NDE, Jung had discovered the profound role of spirituality in mental development. That discovery took him down a path that few others in the world of human psychology would consciously have taken.

I too had had an NDE and went down a spiritual path I would not otherwise have consciously taken. And now my friend Naresh was going down the path too. Like the millions of others who have had mystical experiences, we were all guided to follow a dharma that would lead us in new and surprising directions.

As Jung wrote in *Psychology and Religion* about the gifts of life that are taken for granted, "We are so hemmed in by things which jostle and oppress that we never get a chance, in the midst of all these 'given' things, to wonder by whom they are 'given.' It is from this world of 'given' things that the dead man liberates himself; and the purpose [of life] is to help him towards this liberation."

I would say that Naresh felt greatly liberated by the change in our relationship and the focus of our conversations, and it was a relief to both of us.

A few days before Naresh went in for his surgery, we had lunch together. He was not feeling well. His skin and eyes had the yellow pallor of someone with serious liver problems. He had lost weight and had little energy. Still, he was there at lunch, ready to talk.

I don't remember the particulars of our conversation other than that it dealt with the similar view of the afterlife that seems to exist among all religions, from Christian to Hindu to Muslim.

All of these religions have a core belief about the afterlife that is very similar. I know we wondered how and why this could be and settled on the idea that people of all cultures have similar mystical experiences guiding them down the path of spiritual discovery.

On that day, Naresh thanked me for openly discussing my NDE with him. It would be gross overstatement to say that the story of my NDE had relieved his fears. That would not be possible. Naresh was facing life-threatening cancer surgery, and even if he survived, it would take time to tell if the surgery had gotten rid of the cancer. Naresh had a lot to fear. But still he was appreciative of the story I had shared with him.

"You've given me comfort," he said. "I hope I can do the same for you someday."

I wished the same thing back. But how could I know that such a thing would actually happen?

Chapter 17

Guidance

Despite my attempts to keep it quiet, word of my near-death experience was sweeping the hospital. Although many didn't understand its full scope, it was known that I'd had some kind of transcendent experience during my surgery and was thinking about leaving my post as chief anesthesiologist to "pursue other interests." Although few knew what those "other interests" might be, some guessed. Knowing I'd had some issues with pain pills and antidepressants, a colleague guessed that the meds had finally gotten to me. I wasn't offended by his comment. Such an idea made perfect sense, especially given my own concerns about using prescription drugs in the operating room. The idea that a doctor at my level was leaving for mystical reasons inspired some odd responses. Others spoke about my NDE in other, more positive terms.

"I hear you're hanging up your scrubs," declared one of the senior surgical nurses.

"Maybe," I said, taken by surprise at his openness. "I'm thinking about it."

"Yeah, well, I heard what happened," he said. "It should happen to more doctors because a little more empathy around here wouldn't hurt."

He went on to tell me about some of the patients he had spoken to after their NDEs in our hospital. When he told the doctors about them, they ignored the positive effects these NDEs had on the patients and suggested instead that they talk to a psychologist or to the hospital chaplain or give them meds that would make remembering the experience impossible.

"Why don't you become a chaplain?" asked another nurse. When I told her I was a Hindu and there probably wouldn't be much demand for my services, she shrugged. "We all go to the same place as far as I can tell. It shouldn't really make any difference what religion you are."

Like these veteran nurses, many at the hospital were supportive and nonjudgmental. When I told the hospital administrator about my experience, he listened with rapt attention and then expressed compassion when I told him I was planning to leave and follow the advice of the angels.

"No matter who you are, nothing says you can't experiment with your life," he said. "I just want you to know that you are welcome back anytime you want."

There were also negative comments that, in retrospect, were not meant to be negative, just "good advice." One of my colleagues told me bluntly that I should "get a grip" and "get past" my visionary encounter. Another declared I was "throwing my education down the toilet." A third angrily stated the unthinkable: I was ruining my family.

That last comment touched on one of my greatest fears. I was most concerned about the reaction of the family. I could recover from everything else, but not a broken family. And to be honest, there were certainly signs of stress on the home front.

My wife was still dazed by the change in her husband. She alternately loved and hated the idea of moving to the lesser house we had traded for our mansion. Many of her uncertain feelings related to a loss in status, and to be honest, it affected me as well. By downsizing to the extent we planned, we had concerns that we would no longer be in the epicenter of medical royalty, the top doctors in a community who show up regularly on the society pages of the newspaper. We had always made fun of fitting into this wealthy and educated elite, but now that we might voluntarily be leaving it, we both realized we would miss it.

"It's like taking a voluntary demotion," said Arpana, as we sat on the back porch of our mansion, admiring the view of the golf course that we would soon be without.

But her feelings about change also related to the rapid change she had seen in me. The change in me happened as quickly as a stroke, she said, and sometimes she couldn't tell if it was just a stroke of some kind or a genuine "stroke of insight."

"The man I drove to the emergency room in Los Angeles is not the man I came back with," she said one evening when we were talking about the changes coming into our life. "I both like and fear the new Rajiv and all the changes."

The same was true of our (then) teenage daughter, Ambika. We had not talked to her in detail about my NDE. Being overly protective parents, we thought it might be more information than she could handle. But one day she happened by the kitchen when Arpana and I were talking about the experience, and rather than stopping the conversation, we decided to include her. Before long, she was deeply engrossed in the story and very understanding of the transformational experience that had taken place. She had never heard of NDE and was dumbfounded at first, but she heard the entire story, including the future painted by the angels and how I should change my profession from anesthesiologist to practitioner of consciousness-based healing.

She knew a change was coming, she said, she just didn't expect it to come so quickly. But when we told her that we had agreed to swap our house for a smaller one, she became concerned.

"Why are things changing in our house?" she said fearfully.

"Because I was told to do this by angels during an experience that is beyond this world," I said. "It is an experience that has transformed me and will transform all of us."

Only then did she claim my experience had been a dream or a hallucination. She thought I would forget it, or at least tell the angels I would follow their orders at a later date, perhaps when she was out of the house and off to college.

"This is going to affect my whole life!" she said, looking at me and then her mother. "Mom, this is really going to change *your* whole life."

My sons had a similar reaction. When I came back from the hospital, neither wanted to hear about my experience. My younger son, Arjun, had the sentiments one could expect from almost any young adolescent: He considered the event to be somewhat interesting but almost inconceivable. Most important for him was that news of the event did not leak out. He was clearly interested in making certain that nothing rocked his world.

Our eldest child, Raghav, had a response of almost total indifference, not only to my near-death experience but to me in general. It was what we had both come to expect. Ours had always been a difficult relationship, as relationships between fathers and sons often are. I accepted a certain amount of friction, which I had witnessed in most of my friends' relationships with their sons. We had all talked about our relationships with our sons and come to the conclusion that contention was normal between fathers and sons. One of my doctor friends compared it to the animal kingdom, in which younger lions fight with their fathers for control of the pride.

"I hate it," said my friend. "But I feel the same push against him that he feels against me. I think it's in our DNA, and there's nothing we can do about it. We are made to compete with our male offspring."

I grudgingly agreed, but what I didn't tell my colleagues was that my relationship with Raghav had degenerated far beyond just being genetic rivals. We had become expectational rivals. *I* wanted him to be a medical doctor and *I* pushed him in that direction as hard as I could. Never mind what he wanted. I don't even think I knew what *he* wanted.

In fact it enraged me, and with that rage came a radical personality change: I became angry like my father, that I was not getting the status symbol I wanted—a son who was a medical doctor. "Don't you realize how important this is!" I shouted one time into the phone when he expressed disinterest in his medical studies. But what I could not see was what was important to him. I began to talk to him in ways that a caring father should never speak to his son. I could recount the harsh and mean words I used to "encourage" him in his effort to get through medical school. Let me just say that they have stuck in my mind.

Like my father had done to me and his father to him, I had become verbally abusive to Raghav. Sadly I remember every time I yelled at my son because they are burned into my mind like self-inflicted wounds. To even read them on the page would shame me. It is a forewarning of how our own unfortunate past can exist like a hidden reflex.

I know Raghav feared me, and I think he detested me too. In the little time I spent with him after my NDE, we never once discussed it. I know he spoke to Arpana about it during one of her frequent telephone calls to him in Aruba, where he had attended school, but she never told me what he said. I had the sense that he didn't care much and didn't truly believe that I'd had any kind of conversion experience that would in any way affect our relationship in a positive way. In his eyes I was an ogre, someone angry and alien who could not be pleased, a father who saw him more as a possession than a son.

If that was his vision of me, I now knew it was correct. I had not treated my son admirably. In fact I had not treated anyone in my family admirably. *It is not following the guidance from my near-death experience that might ruin my family*, I thought. *It would be to continue as I had, with very little true spiritual guidance at all!*

––––––––

We were going to be moving to the smaller house in a few days at the same time I was planning to resign my position at the hospital. I was genuinely concerned about the change coming in my life. Even though a Being of Light and two powerful angels had told me what my future should hold and how to attain it, I was still concerned about making the changes they had outlined that would take me to the next step in my spiritual development.

I decided to meditate and ask the universe for guidance. What I received instead was an angelic course in the true meaning of guidance.

Since my return home, I had meditated daily, sometimes several times a day. I was no stranger to meditation. I had practiced it avidly as a young man and credit it with breaking the stress spiral that I experienced in medical school and had caused so many of my fellow students to drop out of their studies. But where I was accustomed to the depths of mindfulness meditation, where I focused on being in the now, I was not used to angels appearing to me, which was what had been happening since my experience.

And so it was on this day. I closed my eyes and settled into a meditative state, letting thoughts come and go with no judgment, just peaceful, like waves in the ocean. Then as I was about to drift into nothingness, I asked the universe for guidance in my decisions about the future.

A familiar voice spoke as the angels materialized in my meditation.

"Guidance doesn't mean what he thinks," said Raphael.

"We need to tell him," said Michael.

"Guidance doesn't mean what you think," said Michael again, speaking directly to me. "Guidance is just a road map, a way to get where you want to go. We've already given you the road map."

"What you are looking for is a guide, someone to take you by the hand and make you follow the road map," said Raphael. "We won't do that. You have to take responsibility for following our guidance and getting yourself there."

The information came to me so fast from the angels that I can only now paraphrase it. Almost everyone has guidance. It's a natural instinct and generally revolves around a "God-given" sense of right and wrong. So it isn't lack of guidance that keeps people from doing the right thing; it's lack of self-reliance and fortitude that keeps us from reaching the goals established in our sense of guidance.

The angels only told me what I should do to have a fulfilling and valuable life, they said. It was up to me to follow their guidance. They were there to talk to me anytime I needed them. Since I had crossed into the spiritual world during the surgery, meditation would allow me to go back in and see them. And if I wanted, they would provide me with guidance. But it was only guidance and inspiration. I didn't have to do what they suggested because it was only a suggestion, not a command.

The guidance I received was essential: Don't do things that destroy your spirit. Treat your physical body like a temple. Respect the differences in others. Love your family and others as you love yourself. I was free to not follow their suggestions, said Michael, because I was a creature with free will.

"Many people choose not to follow our guidance," said Raphael.

"Too many," agreed Michael.

If I chose to follow the guidance I received during my experience, I would help other people find their way, Raphael told me. But there was more than that.

"You will find your own way too."

Chapter 18

What Now?

The conversation I had with the angels about guidance freed my soul. I realized my life was not preordained and I was not being forced to make the changes suggested to me by the spiritual beings I had encountered. Rather, they were providing guidance in the form of advice and not orders.

I was free to do as I wanted. *Free!*

This realization of free will told me that the mistakes I had made thus far in my life had not been preprogrammed to teach me a lesson. I realized I had always received valuable guidance through my own intuition and from others whom I respected. I had also received guidance from those who did wrong, a sort of reverse guidance in which I could experience someone else's bad decision or harsh judgment and correct my own course in life. Many would say, for example, that it was on the day that my father beat me that I formed an inner determination to never again be humiliated or "beaten" by anything or by anyone.

There is another similar event I remember clearly as being a defining moment in my youth.

My mother had arrived at my school for a parent-teacher conference just four weeks after my father had started tutoring me. The reports on me were far from excellent. At some point during the conference, my mother said that she hoped one day I would become a medical doctor. The principal laughed with scorn. Loudly, and angrily, he said to her: "Do you really think your son could *ever* be a doctor?"

My mother was so humiliated and embarrassed by his public dressing down that she began to cry. I watched at her side, horrified by what she was experiencing because of me. I knew the principal was correct about my chances of getting into medical school. At that time in my life, I was clearly headed down an academic path that would take me nowhere near the field of medical studies. But I felt it was very wrong on his part to humiliate my beloved mother.

It was on that day, as a result of the bad example the principal set, that I decided I would *absolutely* become a doctor and that my mother would never be spoken to again like that on my account. I was a sixteen-year-old with below-average grades, but I decided on that day that I would turn myself around and one day my mother would get to see me as a doctor.

By the time I was seventeen, I managed to get offers from two medical schools and started my studies in New Delhi.

My conversation about guidance from the angels made me realize that neither of these events was preordained. Rather, my own drive to become an achiever was an expression of free will. And the realization that I was in a state of free will was an inspiration to accept the guidance provided me by the spiritual beings.

After I accepted their guidance, change happened fast.

The hospital anesthesiologists were having a dinner that week to discuss business. As we did every three months, we gathered in a private room at an upscale Mexican restaurant in the city. There, one of our group would make an informal presentation of the financial picture for the previous quarter while we sipped margaritas. We cared mainly about the bottom line—how much money each of us would make—which the speaker always mentioned within the first thirty seconds of his presentation. After that we heard very little as our subconscious minds spent the money that would roll into our lives like a big green avalanche.

So it went this time. We all took our places at the table and listened happily to the group leader as he revealed an excellent financial quarter. When he finished speaking and after everyone ordered their meals, I asked if I could say a few words.

My palms felt sweaty, and I must have look deeply concerned because a couple of the doctors who usually talk through the presentations fell silent. Their silence made me even more nervous. I didn't like public speaking anyway, and to talk about quitting my job for spiritual reasons and personal health is the kind of resignation that would make anybody in my position nervous.

I cleared my throat.

"I'm quitting my job today," I said. "You probably all know about the spiritual experience I had during surgery. Now I want to make a change in my life."

All of the anesthesiologists had heard about my experience, from friends or nurses at the hospital or from me personally. None seemed terribly surprised, but one of them, a partner in a pain clinic we had started outside the hospital, asked if I was going to continue to work at the anesthesiology group.

"No," I said. "I am going to focus on consciousness-based healing, particularly in the areas of addiction, depression, and chronic pain. I'm going to put meditation and other forms of healing on the front line. I'm not saying pain medications don't have a place, but they won't be the first things I reach for in this healing modality."

I wanted to say more about pain clinics and how they are operated, but they already knew the truth. They knew, as did I, that the pain meds we administer often become the problem rather than the solution, alleviating pain in the short run while causing addictions in the long run. Addiction to prescription pain pills is the number one addiction in America, and many of those dependencies develop in pain clinics.

It would be easy to blame these addiction problems on the medical establishment, which tends to overtreat pain with powerful medications, but it wouldn't be totally fair. Although much chronic pain can be treated with much less pain medication (or none at all), most patients want these medications in order to have a quick fix. They don't want to lose weight, meditate, or exercise to stop their pain. And the doctors? They want to satisfy the patient and, they hope, heal them with the procedures and drugs they are trained to use. It's a given that the more patients they treat, the more money the doctors make. And the more procedures they do, like administering pain meds to a precise spot with a needle, the more that insurance companies pay. In a capitalistic society, why should doctors not want the financial rewards their patients want? The problem is that mixing money and medicine too often results in a sad spiral that can end in addiction and depression for the patient and considerable frustration for conscientious doctors.

I could have addressed these issues, but I didn't want to do so at that time. I was simply there to quit my job.

There was a brief period of silence, and then I heard a number of comments: "Don't throw it away." "Don't give up your degree to become a guru." "You must be kidding!" and even, "I know Raj. He's going into the stock market." And so it went, all through dinner.

It was clear that I would be welcomed back into the group if I decided to return. But there was no way I could see that happening in the foreseeable future. I was leaving traditional medicine for a new specialty: healer of the soul. I was going to fight chronic pain, addiction, and depression—illnesses I had battled for many years. I was going to do it as a practitioner of consciousness-based healing, a form of medicine that had been assigned to me by a pair of angelic beings. It was now up to me to define it and develop treatment methods. From it would emerge a world of possibilities that would provide a new way to practice medicine.

I was thrilled and frightened at the same time. My mind was occupied by one question: *What do I do now?*

Chapter 19

Funeral for Myself

What do I do now?

It was the next morning, and I was lying in bed watching the room light up with the sunrise. I looked at the clock and saw that it was shortly after 6:30. This had been the time I arose for work, and I felt a brief jolt of nervous energy at thinking that I needed to be on my feet and headed toward the shower. *But that was before my NDE and before I quit my job,* I thought. Today was a new day and a new life.

I lay on my back and thought about that last day. My colleagues at the hospital had mixed reactions at the realization that I was truly leaving. Some of them approached with great sincerity and shook my hand and wished me well. Others slapped me on the back and assured me I would return to the hospital in no time, as though I had some kind of temporary illness.

"Once you spend a few days at home, you'll just be floating around aimlessly and uncomfortably, wondering just what the hell you're going to do next," said one of our surgeons. "That's when you'll come back."

Now I could hear his words as though he were right there in the room with me, and I answered in kind, saying out loud, "What do I do now?"

"I have a few ideas," said Arpana, coming out of the closet wearing a lovely blue dress that she would change out of at her dental office in favor of a pair of surgical scrubs. "You can take my car in for its twenty-thousand-mile checkup. That'll eat up much of the morning."

I saw the humor in what she said and chuckled. Overnight I had become the person responsible for the chores rather than the paycheck. Arpana no longer feared that we would be forced to downsize to a much smaller house. Our house trade with the plastic surgeon was now a reality, and we were ready to move out of the mansion that had sucked our money the way a black hole sucks energy. My expensive cars had been traded, or would soon be, leaving us both to wonder why we hadn't gone for the less expensive models to begin with. I, who once drove a gas-guzzling Hummer, was now driving a hybrid Camry, which moved my life literally and figuratively from Hummer to hybrid. And our children grudgingly accepted the fact that less money would be spent on their schooling and "extra expenses."

In a matter of months, we had confronted our materialism and won. By talking rationally and separating our needs from our wants, we had changed the nature of our egos by 180 degrees. Rather than needing more to feel good about ourselves, we discovered the wisdom of less. We found that needs are far less expensive than wants and that we could be happy in a less materialistic world that did not depend on the ego gratification of bling.

The friends we expected to lose through our new outlook on life remained friends. I am sure they gossiped about us, but that's normal human behavior, so we didn't really care. It's what they said to our face that mattered most, and what they usually expressed was envy at what they perceived to be courage in the face of a social downgrade.

"I wish we could do what you've done," said one of my colleagues. "We're so caught up in it that we can't escape."

"Status is an illness, just like cancer," said a friend from our soon-to-be old neighborhood. "It eats away at you, and it's hard to stop."

"The deeper in debt we get, the deeper we go," said another neighbor, whose garage looked like a luxury car lot.

And then there was my friend Naresh, whose cancer was not getting better. We still had lunch often, during which our conversations became more reflective of the lives we were living.

"It's too late to change now, but I wish I had given more to the needy than being so concerned about making more money," said Naresh. "I wish I had devoted more time to service."

"It's not too late," I said to my dying friend.

"It's too late, of that I'm sure," said Naresh. "Change is for the future, and I don't have much future left."

At the conferences I attended, people spoke to us freely, revealing their darkest spiritual fears as though I was their confessor. These conversations made me realize how correct the Being of Light had been to focus on the disease of materialism. I realized it needed to be a major focus in my study of consciousness-based healing.

What do I do now?

The thought of consciousness-based healing made me realize how little I knew about whatever this form of medicine was. *How do I figure out my new role in life, in my God-given dharma?*

I could hear Arpana moving around the kitchen getting ready

to leave for work. As I got up to join her for a cup of tea, I remembered the kindness of her response when I told her I would have to leave anesthesiology to practice a form of medicine that wasn't yet clear to me.

"You have taken good care of us all of these years," she had said. "I'll support the family while you find the meaning of your higher path. You will still be a good father and husband, a better one even, if you do what you need to do."

I retrieved my robe from the closet and headed down the stairs, but before I reached the landing, she was out the garage door and on her way to work.

I was alone.

What do I do now?

I had an idea: *I will hold a funeral for myself!*

I had discovered such a concept years earlier when I escaped medical school and fled temporarily to the Ramakrishna ashram in the Himalayas. There I was surrounded by Hindu monks in their orange robes who seemed overwhelmingly happy to be alive and fully occupied in the moment. They were the most free people I had ever seen, yet they were confined for the rest of their lives within the walls of the ashram. *How can they be so happy?* I wondered. *Certainly they must have had a different upbringing than I did.*

Compelled by curiosity I asked several of the monks what their childhoods were like. Expecting their lives to be pure and ideal, I was surprised to hear that some had had miserable childhoods of poverty and abuse. Yet when they told me their stories, they smiled. I asked one of the monks how he left the past behind.

"Pain is inevitable; suffering is optional," he said, meaning that we don't have to hold on to thoughts that cause us to suffer.

I asked another monk how he had left his past behind. Wasn't he angry at the pain that had been inflicted on him as a child?

"I have learned to let go of anger," he said in the giggly, carefree way of many Hindu monks. "The Buddha said that 'holding on to anger is like grasping a hot coal with the intent of throwing it at someone else. It's you who gets burned first.'"

All of them referred to a ceremony they had performed to purge them of their past. In everyday parlance, it was called "a funeral for myself." It is done by all new Hindu monks to clear them of their past, whether it be good or bad, and give them a rebirth into the world so their new spiritual beliefs can fully occupy their heart and soul. In essence, they become new people, spiritually reborn fresh.

I discovered later that monks and nuns in many religions carry out such ceremonies. Most who go through this ceremony sever connections with their past and are rarely, if ever, allowed to communicate with their family and friends. They turn themselves over to the spiritual life totally. That is how serious they are about attaining a spiritual existence.

I had no interest in disavowing my family. I knew that I was nothing without my family, just as I knew that I had some healing to do within it. But I was interested in acknowledging that I had become a new man who had to leave some of my past behind to carry out the spiritual mission I had been assigned.

With that in mind, I decided to perform a funeral for myself right there in the backyard of our palatial mansion at the center of the bull's-eye. I gathered together all of my surgical clothing from my closet and folded them carefully to show respect for what they represented. To that I added stock market books from my gambling period, some bottles of pain pills to represent my addiction, magazine ads of cars I wanted to buy, a photo of my father from the period in our life that I wanted to forget, and other objects and images that were better left in ashes.

I carried this pile to the backyard and stacked it carefully in the barbecue. I squeezed a can of lighter fluid and doused the items with a stream of the flammable liquid and struck a match. When the fumes reached the fire, my past exploded in a ball of flame. I couldn't have been happier.

I sat and stared, entranced by the fire as it consumed my past. I had several disjointed thoughts, all of them good. I thought of my mother and her happiness at my graduation from medical school; of my father who learned to accept his own life and therefore mine; of my eldest son, whom I loved deeply despite our struggles; and of my wife, who accepted with love and grace the changes my NDE demanded. I thought of many things, all good, and I no longer feared the future. I felt chosen.

I thought again of the ashram in the Himalayas, the one to which I had fled as a young man to escape the rigors of medical school. When I arrived, I told the guru that I wanted to become a holy man and leave behind the world as I knew it. He only laughed and told me I was not ready.

Now I had fled my life again, this time at the behest of a Being of Light, two angels, and a mystical exploration that was truly profound.

I had to laugh at the notion that I had come over thirty years and halfway around the world to now begin my studies as a holy man. I wondered what the guru would say if he saw me now, an older version of myself making a surprise return to the spiritual realm, this time at the request of angels. In the flaming embers of my past life, I could see him, a big Hindu smile on his face as he asked, *Are you ready now?*

I was startled to realize that the answer was no. I still felt a need to clean up my past, forgive God for the pain that had been inflicted on me, forgive my father for the abuse he had heaped on me, and finally forgive myself for the trespasses I had heaped on others.

To wipe the slate clean, I decided to write letters to God, my father, and myself. I went to my home office and took several sheets of stationery from my drawer and began writing.

First the letter to God:

Dear Divine,

I "forgive you," for I have been angry with You. So much I often denied Your very existence. I was mad at You for the way You made my life change for the worse. Why did I have to suffer from cancer, from so many surgeries and their complications like incontinence and impotency? Why did I have to suffer from depression, addiction, and chronic pain? Why did I have to lose money by gambling in the stock market? Why did I have to endure abuse in my childhood?

Now I understand Your love for me. All of what is mentioned above, and other things were preparing me for a higher cause so I could serve humanity, especially people suffering from pain, depression, anger, and addictions. It was to make me stronger, a pillar for others.

I am grateful for all I had to go through, especially my NDE, where I experienced true unconditional, supreme love. I am grateful for all of the blessings I have in my life, my family and friends, the roof over my head, and the food I have. Now I understand that this grief represents an opportunity. Now that I have experienced the bad I can now understand it and spread your message of "forgiveness, love, and healing" to millions.

I ask for forgiveness and seek Your blessings so I can be a strong, passionate messenger.

With deep humble respects,
Rajiv

The letter to my father came next.

Dear Father,

When I saw you during my near-death experience, you revealed much to me about why you behaved so abusively toward me during my childhood.

I had known about your unhappy youth, but I now see and feel what you suffered as if I shared it with you. Harshness was your defense, your shield against unloving, abusive parents and historical events that forced you to endure years of humiliation.

How painful it must have been to be the eldest of four sons but the least appreciated because your skin was so much darker and your features not as handsome. How it must have broken your heart to cut short your education and to sacrifice your future so that you could support your father and brothers instead of going to university.

Your desire to hide your pain hardened your heart. You sometimes mocked or swore at me. If I cried, you would laugh at me and say that strong boys do not cry. I had to harden my own heart against you, often hating you as you hated your father. As an adult, when I longed to ask you why you were so unloving during my early years, I dared not. My childhood fears of your anger and sarcasm overcame my courage even then.

Though I understand that you treated me as your father treated you only because you knew no other way to love me, my feelings about you remain unsettled. It was your dream to go to medical school. Did I go to please you and win your love and approval or was it my choice? I honestly don't know the answer.

On one hand, I know I loved being a doctor—that it satisfied my passion for learning and helping others. On the other hand, if I did go to please you, I fear that every father will spank the hell out of his son to make him a doctor.

So it is that we have danced between yin and yang, light and dark, good and bad, love and hate. To this day, if I dream about you, I feel fear. Yet, how could you know about the power of kindness when you'd been given so little?

It's now time that I make a choice, a choice you gave me when we met in the afterlife. It's now time to replace these painful memories of anger and fear with the better ones where you stopped being violent and became more loving. Do you remember them?

Mother showed you how to help me and you did. You used to awaken me at 4 a.m. and make me coffee and sandwiches while I studied. Soon my grades rose and with it my standing in class. By the time I graduated from high school I was selected by two medical schools. In a competitive country where only 1 in 100,000 students is selected for medical school, that was quite an accomplishment. I thank you—you taught me to excel at my studies.

I learned much from you about hard work, focus, and respect. For years, I have worn one of your shirts on important days when I am to be "tested" or challenged and need to feel your faith in me.

Even as a young husband and father, you envisioned the importance of the future. Because of your farsightedness about investments, my mother's future is financially secure and so are those of your children.

Please forgive me for arousing your worst fears with my childhood disobedience and for my self-centered adulthood when I, too, unjustly punished my children with the anger you and I shared.

I forgive you for every cruel word and every raised hand. I forgive you for the abuse and thank you for your love, unexpressed though it often was.

You wisely told me during my NDE that anger was a choice. I now choose that the anger that plagued our family shall stop with me.

With Love and Forgiveness,
Rajiv

Then came the most difficult letter of all, the one to myself. In order for my confession to be effective, I had to be totally honest about my failings.

Dear Rajiv,

I forgive you for the many failings in your life and am proud of your courage to expose them to the light.

- *I forgive you for the way in which you have treated your children, especially your eldest son Raghav. You have often exposed your angry side to them but most of all Raghav, who you expected to follow in your footsteps instead of truly helping him find a career to match his desires and his intellect.*
- *I forgive you for becoming addicted to pain medications and for not choosing a holistic path on which the pain could be controlled in a more healthy way.*
- *I forgive you for treating your patients like they were beneath you. You were not kind.*
- *I forgive you for following the God of materialism, wasting your money on a big house, expensive cars and other objects of desire rather than using your wealth to help the poor.*
- *I forgive you for treating your wife poorly, sometimes more like an object than your most important friend. I hope she forgives you too.*
- *I forgive you for lack of faith.*
- *I forgive you for not being grateful for your blessings and instead acting like you deserved them and more.*

- *I forgive you for not living in integrity with your higher truth.*
- *I forgive you for not fulfilling your promise to God.*

With Truth about myself,
Rajiv

With the letters completed, I took them outside to the barbecue where the objects representing my life were still smoldering. One by one, I read each letter out loud. After reflecting on the content, I tore each letter into four pieces and tossed it on the fire. When one letter had turned to ash, I went on to the next.

Forgive, love, and heal.

As I tore up the second letter, I heard the words *forgive, love, and heal.* I looked around, but there was no one, not even a golfer passing on the course, yet the words were loud and clear.

Forgive, love, and heal.

The fact that I had heard them in a mystical way told me I should pay attention. With pen and paper in hand, I wrote the words *Forgive . . . Love . . . Heal* at the top of three pieces of paper. Then I wrote the first things that came to mind about each of the words. The result was a clear understanding of the words that would form the core goal of consciousness-based healing: *Forgive, love, heal.*

+ *Forgive*: Most of us think that we have been wronged somewhere in our life. Whether it's a mother who was mean, a father who was abusive, a job we didn't get because of some wrongdoing, or a sense that God didn't deliver what we prayed for. No matter what the case, these wrongs fester in our mind, taking up brain power that could be used for more positive things. But by clearly defining those wrongs, one can examine them closely and see them as roadblocks to emotional growth.

   By writing letters of forgiveness, I can actually visualize the issues to be forgiven on the page. When I burn the letter, I can see the issues going up in smoke. It's a reminder to me that nothing lasts forever, and that bad moments from the past should not be left in the way of my future.

I want to add that "forgiveness" does not mean "forgetting." Some trespasses cannot be forgotten. But when you practice forgiveness you allow the physical body, the heart, and the soul to heal. But when you are stuck in anger, you are totally empty. It's the spiritual and emotional equivalent of a physical healing, akin to breaking a bone and having it heal.

+ *Love*: Love is the underlying true nature of all things, including "even humans" as archangel Michael put it. Science has revealed this, showing that the further we humans move away from feeling love, the more resentful, unforgiving, isolated, and negative we become, and the more rapid our degeneration toward disease. On the other hand, the more we cultivate compassion, love, and forgiveness, the more we experience healing and well-being.

  Feeling a true sense of love for a person who has done you wrong is not easy (as I found out in my own life), but if you can do so, it confirms the old adage that "the true resolution of grief is to love unconditionally."

+ *Heal*: It makes sense to me that when we clear up various emotional issues, it helps the body relax and cure itself. I have seen people heal when they confront their emotions and let past fear and resentments go. I have concluded that negative emotions like the failure to forgive release chemicals in the body that, while useful in the short run, are destructive in the long run. Our subconscious brain remains constantly on alert for threats to our survival. When we have been wronged or harmed, it fires off signals to alert the rest of our body to protect against the perceived danger. Adrenaline pumps through the body, breathing gets shallower, and blood rushes to our limbs and away from our internal organs. This is appropriate for the initial threat, but when a negative emotion like unforgiveness replays the incident over and over, these reactions become toxic.

At the deepest level, the basis of everything is raw energy and light. Spiritual traditions have known this for centuries and modern scientists are now able to observe and validate its truth. Also, at the quantum level, everything is connected—not just everything in your own system but everything in the universe. So there is no way that your emotional life is separate from your physical health!

In simple terms (which is how I understood it at the time) the basis of everything in our body is raw energy, and negative emotions are "black balloons" of energy that need to be punctured to keep from doing damage. If they aren't dissipated in some way, they can help create a variety of illnesses, including:

+ Depression
+ Drug and alcohol addiction
+ Binge eating
+ Smoking
+ Stress
+ Loneliness
+ Asthma
+ Skin disorders
+ Gastrointestinal issues like irritable bowel syndrome

Those were the explanations I wrote down for the words of my core message: *Forgive, love, and heal.*

I had received a substantial amount of information from the Being of Light during my NDE, information I was supposed to use to clarify the meaning of consciousness-based healing. Yet I didn't remember all of the information when I came back from my experience, a great source of frustration for me. After all, I was supposed to create a practice dedicated to a form of medicine I didn't know or understand.

Still, the angels said they would be with me as guides. And on this particular day, they were. It was as though holding a funeral for myself represented a turning point, a sort of crossing of the Rubicon that meant I would not turn back and join my old life but was somehow changed forever. On the afternoon of my first official day as a consciousness-based healer, Michael and Raphael returned to provide important guidance.

Sometimes their appearances were very conversational or even humorous and playful. Today it was none of those. As I sat cross-legged in my meditation room, the angels suddenly appeared. They said nothing. Rather, they were present just briefly before evaporating from my mental eyesight. But in the time they were there, a telepathic transmission of information took place that gave me further clues as to the focus and structure of consciousness-based healing.

When I came out of my meditation, I hurried back to the writing desk and wrote down seven basic truths that I have come to call "The Near-Death Manifesto."

1. Consciousness can exist outside the body.
2. There is life after death.
3. We have past lives, and our experiences therein can shape our current realities.

4. We are all connected to each other because we are all made of the one and same energy that manifests as differentiated matter.
5. Divine beings exist to help and guide us.
6. There are different levels of consciousness.
7. There is one, all-pervading, supreme love and intelligence that is the source of the entire universe, and that love is the supreme source of creation.

The seven points of the Near-Death Manifesto were enormously helpful in understanding the concepts of consciousness-based healing. And although I didn't feel the seven points were specific enough, I also remembered what the Being of Light had said to me when I begged for information about consciousness-based healing. *You have the knowledge,* said the Being. *You have been humbled by pain, so you have the knowledge. But you must teach yourself; all people must teach themselves. Finding your own knowledge inside you is the best way to learn. If you don't learn for yourself, you will not learn completely.*

I wanted more information as I had from the beginning. But I also knew that the information would come to me as I needed it. I accepted that the unfolding of information was not for me to control.

More than ever before, I felt it was important to do what I had been instructed to do, and that left me frightened. In order to become a healer of the soul, I would have to do the thing that frightened me most: speak in public.

I could imagine what the Being of Light had shown me already: crowds of hundreds of people with me standing in front of them, fearlessly telling my story and explaining how they could cure the diseases of their soul by following my advice.

I was not frightened when the Being of Light allowed me to see my public-speaking performances in the near future. But that was during my experience with a powerful spiritual Being at my side. Now I was alone with no spiritual Being in sight and the idea of speaking in public to hundreds of people made me feel ill. Plus, what would I talk to them about? Beyond my NDE and the information the Near-Death Manifesto gave me, I didn't feel as though I could be enlightening enough to inspire a group of spiritually ill people.

Still, I knew the next step was the public podium. That is what I was told to do, and that is what I would do. My life was going to change, and I was changing with it. The Being of Light said so.

The Near-Death Manifesto that the angels had delivered during meditation was the bare bones of consciousness-based healing and the next step in my education. But it was clear that to fully understand the seven elements of the manifesto, I had to take them to the people. I had to tell my story in public and do so in a fearless and confident manner. If I told my story well, then people with addiction, depression, and chronic pain would fill in the blanks and help me understand how to treat diseases of the soul. Consciousness-based healing, it seemed, was a crowd-sourced medicine in which those with the need would let me know how to fulfill them. This information would come to me out of the depths of the human soul.

If there is one thing all people want, it is to be understood. And if there is a thing people respond to, it is a fellow human's desire to understand them. When people realize someone is seeking to understand them, defensive behaviors drop and they reveal truths about themselves that they have kept hidden for years. Seeking understanding is the basis of love, beyond which comes acceptance and healing.

I think the need for understanding is basic human nature. And this nature has been expressed by all religions in their own way because it is a deeply spiritual need.

Although I am a Hindu, I am somewhat familiar with a few Bible verses, one of which applied very well to the relationship between understanding and revelation of information: "Ask and it shall be given you; seek, and ye shall find; knock, and it shall be open to you." It is a verse from the Book of Matthew that I looked up after hearing it from a surgeon who, forgetting a surgical technique in the midst of surgery, picked up a cell phone and calmly called a fellow surgeon to find out how it should be done. "Ask and it shall be given you," he said after hanging up. It was a verse that applied to his situation and certainly applied to the situation I was in now. Like the surgeon who needed advice at a critical time, I too had to seek out those in need of spiritual healing and discover specifically what they needed in order to recover their spirit. By asking them what they needed, I hoped they would open their hearts and minds.

My NDE and the events that followed had been disrupting to my family, especially to Arpana. Yet rather than reject the experience as a fantasy, she had struggled to understand what had happened both during the experience and in the days after.

I had much to thank Arpana for, and I felt moved to express my appreciation by doing something I had never done before. Later that day I sat at my writing desk and wrote a poem that expressed the true depth of my love.

What Is Love?

Love is
> when you are there, then the world is there; Nirvana—the ultimate bliss—is there.

Love is
> when standing in the DMV line together, a couple has more fun than others have on their honeymoon.

Love is
> when it's like two different flavors of ice cream that want to melt together.

Love is
> when one sleeps and the other, even with a sprained ankle, tiptoes so the other does not wake.

Love is
> when being together is like the smell from the earth when it has been dry and now the first rain falls.

Love is
> when, being together, time stops, and one feels that this is it, heaven.

Love is
> when one's heart skips a beat upon seeing the other.

Love is
> when holding hands and running on the beach feels like being one with the universe.

Love is
  when one feels: I am her, she is me.

Love is
  when one happily gives up one's personal desires for the other
  to be happy.

Love is
  when one feels that on this journey called life, one's soul mate
  has been found.

Love is
  when holding hands feels like walking in spring in a garden
  of fresh flowers, surrounded by their sight and fragrance, and
  by the sound of birds singing.

Love is
  when, in spite of all efforts, including those above, one gives
  up and says: You are love personified. Otherwise, I cannot
  define it.

When I later gave the poem to Arpana, she was deeply moved. She read it twice and then looked up at me with tears in her eyes. "I guess this means you didn't take my car in for its checkup," she said. We both laughed. It was a good day.

Chapter 20

An Awakening

Jo McGinley is an actress and speech coach who reveals the secrets of public speaking from an office in Los Angeles. She came highly recommended to me by an acquaintance who knew that I needed help in speaking to groups larger than two.

My near-death experience and the messages I received were always on my mind. Yet this one—the request by the Being of Light to tell the story of my NDE in public—seemed like a fate worse than death to me.

Jo told me this was a common fear among glossophobics like myself. At least 75 percent of the American public is glossophobic, she said, which means they cannot speak in front of a crowd without fighting a desire to run and hide. And of those, a high percentage in one study admitted they would rather die than speak in public.

Choosing death over public speaking seems a severe reaction, but one I could easily understand. I told her of once going blank

169

in front of a group of high school kids while explaining anesthesia. For a moment or two, I lost my train of thought while the room turned white and my mind went blank. I got back on track quickly, but the fact that it happened did nothing for my confidence.

"That's more common than you might think," said Jo, exhibiting a bright smile and confidence I envied.

After a discussion of public speaking basics ("Don't forget to breathe"; "Make eye contact with the friendly eyes in the audience"; "Don't move around too much"), Jo suggested that I write out a speech and practice it a few times at home before delivering it to her at our next meeting.

I did that, writing the particulars of my NDE in excruciating detail. But no matter how many times I read it, something just wasn't right. There was no spontaneity in my presentation, and I felt as though the written words were holding me back, forcing me to stay glued to them until I sounded like I was delivering a canned speech. Which I was.

On the day of our next appointment, I was nervous. I read what I had written one more time and then drove to Los Angeles for the meeting. When I got there, Jo decided to trick me.

"Did you write out a speech?" she asked.

I held it up, a bundle of pages for her to see.

"Good," she said, taking the pages away from me. "Just tell me the story. Speak from your heart."

My first instinct was to bolt from the room. My second was to fight back against the fight-or-flight reaction I was having: damp palms and racing heartbeat. Instead I took a deep breath and told my story.

I started with my chronic wrist pain, then my prostate cancer and the decline of my physical health. I spoke about my many surgeries to cope with the problems caused by the cancer, and the abdominal surgery during which I left my body and had the experience that was transcendent and transformative.

I covered that experience in detail, telling about the mystical appearance in India and seeing my mother in the kitchen with my sister at her home in New Delhi. I told about being led from the lip of hell by my deceased father and the family members I met in the tunnel to heaven who allowed me to understand why my father had treated me so poorly. I told her about the guardian angels who have not left me since, and the Being of Light who gave me counsel and whose advice was now leading me down a new path.

I emphasized my rapid healing and cure from addiction to pain pills and how these two events convinced my wife that something truly miraculous had taken place. I told her how my near-death experience had brought such unbelievable love into my life that my friends and family now saw me as a different person.

Many of my relationships have changed, I told her, especially the one with my eldest son. I had been abusive to him in the past. Now, after the NDE, I was trying to be compassionate and helpful. My son welcomed the change in my personality—my whole family did—but it was so radical that it was difficult at times for them to accept.

I told her about leaving my job and searching for ways to help those with diseases of the soul, explaining to her that the Being of Light had told me to relate my story in public and reach more people with a message of healing.

"That is my dharma," I told her. "I am now determined to make the world a better place."

As I spoke, her eyes began to tear up. Then she applauded.

"What you need to do is just speak from the heart," she told me. "Just open your soul and let the story out."

And that's what I did.

When one door closes, another opens, the saying goes. In the next several days, I found out just how true that was. I called several organizations interested in the study of life after death and was immediately signed up as a conference or luncheon speaker for several of them. The ease at which I was accepted made me nervous and somewhat paranoid. *Will they doubt my story? Think I'm crazy? Use me as a punching bag for their skepticism?* I didn't know what to expect, but I knew I had to speak to whatever crowd showed up because that is what the Being of Light had told me to do.

I went to these events with nothing—no notes, no preconceived notions—and when I was called, I walked slowly to the dais and told my story. In essence I went on autopilot, holding nothing back. My goal was simple: to be honest and therefore remove fear, personal doubts, and depression from those who feel the marvel and wonder of life have left them. My goal was not only to confirm the truth of the near-death experience, that there is a rich spiritual life when we die, but that the spiritual life revealed through an NDE can be reached without nearly dying. All it takes is a willingness to seek enlightenment through consciousness-based healing.

When I started speaking to these groups, I didn't completely understand consciousness-based healing myself. But as I continued to make appearances, the people I was speaking to taught me the goals of consciousness-based healing and how to reach it. As the Being of Light had told me, *the healing of these diseases can be achieved only through consciousness.* The more I spoke and read, the more I realized I was tapping into the consciousness of others who had had an NDE. Their stories became like puzzle pieces to me, and it was my goal to assemble those pieces into a comprehensible message that would reveal for me the meaning of consciousness-based healing.

I had no preplanned methodology to gather and dissect the NDEs of others. Instead, after I finished each talk, I was besieged by experiencers who wanted to share their stories and who had usually broken it down to its most relevant message.

At a conference in Southern California, a man told me of having a heart attack and collapsing on a downtown sidewalk. People came to his aid immediately and the emergency medical technicians were called. At the site where he collapsed and on the way to the hospital, a man was with him, a stranger, providing comfort as the EMTs did their work and even in the hospital as the staff prepared to put a stent into the occluded artery that had caused the heart attack. He said, "I thought it was strange that this man appeared as soon as I had my heart attack. He was right there with everyone who stopped on the sidewalk, but he didn't leave my side, even when they loaded me into the ambulance. And no one seemed to notice him or ask him to get out of the way. He was there providing me comfort. He kept saying, 'You'll be okay. This isn't the end for you! Just relax.'"

Later, while lying in recovery, he was visited again by this man who spoke to him, he said, "like an angel" and then left. "I couldn't understand exactly what he said, but his voice and presence was the most soothing encounter I have ever had." When he asked the nurses about the man later, they had no idea who he was talking about.

Even years later, the man who'd had the heart attack sometimes senses the presence of this being. "It's a wonderful feeling to have him around," he told me. "His presence has confirmed two of my beliefs: that guardian angels exist and that there is an afterlife."

A woman at a conference in Phoenix, Arizona, told how she had been running through a playground as a child when she ran straight into a set of metal monkey bars. Here's her story as I remember her telling it:

Everything went black, and when I woke up, I was looking down at myself, flat on my face, surrounded by other girls and boys. Some of the boys started running toward the school office to get help, and others ran to a nearby teacher who had heard my head hit the metal bar.

I tried to speak to my friends and tell them I was all right, but they couldn't hear me. One of the girls below covered her mouth and said, "Oh my God, she's dead!" I yelled that I wasn't dead, that I was sitting up in a tree above them, but there was no tree close to the monkey bars. I was just above the scene and nobody could hear me and I didn't know why. I stayed that way for a long time and then finally woke up inside my body.

When I asked the woman what the experience meant to her, she had an immediate answer: "It changed my life. At a very early age I realized we are two people, physical and spiritual, and the spiritual body doesn't need the physical to survive. Knowing that has made me free."

A story came to me from Dr. Raymond Moody who was at the same conference. He had been studying shared-death experiences (SDEs), a category of experience in which a bystander experiences the NDE of a person who is dying. Although SDEs have long been discussed in the field of near-death studies, Moody began studying them in earnest after his entire family had an SDE at the bedside of his dying mother. Raymond told me about the first SDE he ever heard about and what it meant to him.

He said that he was still in medical school when he wrote his classic book on NDEs, *Life after Life*. One day he was reading a magazine at the university bookstore when a respected member of the faculty—we'll call her Dr. Jamieson—approached him and asked if she could speak to him in private. When they got to her office and sat down, Dr. Jamieson got right to the point.

To begin with, let me tell you that I was not raised in a religious family. That doesn't mean my parents were against religion; they just didn't have an opinion about it. As a result, I never thought about the afterlife because it was not a subject that came up in our household.

Anyway, about two years ago, my mother had a cardiac arrest. It was unexpected and happened at home. I happened to be visiting her when it took place and had to work on her with CPR. Can you imagine what it's like to give your mother mouth-to-mouth resuscitation? It is difficult enough on a stranger, but it was almost inconceivable to do it on my own mother.

I continued to work on her for a long time, maybe thirty minutes or so, until I realized that any further effort was futile and that she was dead. At that point I stopped and caught my breath. I was exhausted, and I can honestly say that it hadn't yet sunk in that I was now an orphan.

Suddenly, Dr. Jamieson felt herself lift out of her body, said Moody. She realized that she was above her own body and the deceased body of her mother, looking down on the whole scene as though she were on a balcony.

"Being out of my body took me aback," she said. "As I was trying to get my bearings, I suddenly became aware that my mother was now hovering with me in spirit form. She was right next to me!"

Dr. Jamieson calmly said good-bye to her mother, who was now smiling and quite happy, a stark contrast to her deceased body below. Then Dr. Jamieson saw something else that surprised her:

"I looked in the corner of the room and became aware of a breach in the universe that was pouring Light like water coming from a broken pipe. Out of that Light came people I had known for years, deceased friends of my mother. But there were other people there as well, people I didn't recognize but I assume they were friends of my mother's that I didn't know."

As Dr. Jamieson watched, her mother drifted off into the Light. The last Dr. Jamieson saw of her mother, she said, was her having a very tender reunion with all of her friends.

"When the Light closed off, the tube closed down in an almost spiral fashion like a camera lens," she said.

How long this all lasted Dr. Jamieson didn't know. But when it ended, she found herself back in her body, standing next to her deceased mother, totally puzzled about what had just happened.

"What do you make of that story?" she asked.

Moody could only shrug. At this point, he had heard dozens of regular near-death experiences and was hearing new ones each week. But there was little about Dr. Jamieson's experience that he could comment on, since this was the first shared-death experience he had ever heard about.

Now, decades later, Dr. Moody has heard many shared-death experiences. I asked him what special meaning they had to him.

"Well, I will tell you a couple of things it means to me," said Moody. "One, it means that somehow we are all connected to one another in an unseen way and in that same unseen way we are linked to God and the universe. Few events would prove that more than a shared-death experience. The other thing is that these experiences are transformative. All of them. Whether they are NDEs or SDEs or the out-of-body experiences people have during meditation, the people who have these experiences are never the same again. They are totally transformed!"

He told one of his favorite stories of transformation at the hands of an SDE, one that happened during World War II to a poet named Karl Skala. He was trapped in a foxhole during an artillery bombardment when one of the shells landed close and killed the soldier who was huddled with Skala. The blast pushed the soldier against Skala, who knew that the young man had been killed by the explosion.

As the bombardment continued, Skala could feel himself being drawn into the heavens with the dead soldier, where they suddenly found themselves looking down onto the battlefield. As Skala held his friend, he looked up and could see a bright Light. The two soldiers moved at a rapid rate toward this Light until Skala suddenly stopped and returned to his body. The blast left Skala nearly deaf for the rest of his life. It also made him far more spiritual.

After the war, the young poet wrote of his experience in a poem that says a lot about the nature of all of these truly incredible experiences, the last lines of which read:

let this light shine deep in your heart, in your dreams
on
this earth.
Death is an awakening.

Death is an awakening.

The more I thought about the last line of Skala's poem, the more I realized its truth. And the more I traveled and spoke, the more stories I heard. And the more stories I heard, the clearer the definition of consciousness-based healing became. This clarity came as a result of talking to those who had crossed the threshold of death and returned to apply their knowledge to the puzzle of earthly life.

As Skala wrote, *Death is an awakening*, or, in the case of the people I spoke to, *near* death is an awakening.

There were two constants with those who had experienced an NDE: they had a profound transformation and a strong desire to return to the state of being they were in during the NDE.

It is clear that having a near-death experience has a profound effect on the rest of a person's life. Many researchers have noticed the transformation that takes place and have identified its elements: a changed self-image that allows them to take a long view of life, increased compassion for others, an appreciation of life that leaves them with a sense that they still have something to accomplish here on earth, a diminished fear of death coupled with a belief in life after death, a decline in religious affiliation while at the same time an increase in spirituality, a sense of greater intuitive sensitivity and heightened sensitivity to the five physical senses (sight, sound, taste, touch, smell).

People who have NDEs don't always present with all of these transformative elements, but they do present with several of them, and they almost always seem somewhat aloof to the world around them. The reason for this aloofness? "We're on earth a short time and then it's off to another destination," said one person who had had an NDE. "So why worry?"

Another constant that was even more intriguing to me was the desire to return to the NDE state, to be able to replicate parts of the NDE or even its whole. Don't confuse this with suicidal tendencies. I have yet to encounter anyone who had an NDE and had a desire to commit suicide. They now know they have work to complete on earth, even if it's just expressing the change that has taken place in their lives. Rather, they want to return to this special state of solace and learning again and again. As one person declared, "A child never wants to go to Disneyland only once."

Having had an NDE myself, I can say it is more complex than that. Where I went was no amusement park. It was a deep dive into my mental self, coupled with a brief glimpse into the world of the spirit, the place we go when we die. It is difficult to say why there is such a powerful need to return to that spiritual state other than to say it had put me on a new path that changed my personality, broke old patterns of living that were detrimental to me and my family, gave me greater compassion for others, and led me on a search for the spiritual instead of the material. Returning to the NDE state was like a course correction to keep me on the righteous path, a compass heading that led me to God.

After months of speaking in venues large and small and hearing the NDEs of others who were so grateful to have a place where they could tell their story freely, I came to a number of conclusions that distilled my approach to consciousness-based healing. These five rules, which I call "Lessons of the Light," gave me a methodology by which to present this form of medicine to a larger audience that is hungry for the benefits of an NDE:

1. *Have a sense of oneness with the universe.* This is one of the most often repeated lessons of the near-death experience and certainly one of its most transformative. The idea that what we do can have a positive effect on the circle of people we influence takes away our sense of powerlessness. The NDE teaches about personal power through this oneness principle. Keep in mind too that when we talk about feeling a oneness with the universe, we are including our sense of gratitude toward the world. Two of the best ways to express gratitude, you already know. One is to stop and smell

the roses, which means to consciously slow down and open ourselves to what we are experiencing at each moment. The world's wonders are more apparent to us if we calm the chatter in our minds. The second is to count our blessings, which means to meditate on what we can be thankful for in our lives.

2. *Turn off the verbal mind*. Communication during the NDE is almost always nonverbal. Most people report telepathic communications with the beings they see during their experience. I know that is how it was for me and still is when my guardian angels communicate with me during meditation.

Turning off the verbal mind can be done in a variety of ways, including the repetition of a single word or mantra, performing a repetitive act like needlework, or, my preferred method, meditation. Perhaps the act of turning off one of my senses opens the others wider. That includes spiritual senses too. When I turn off my verbal mind, I at times solve problems or see places I have been in vivid detail. I will see my guardian angels or even my father or other deceased relatives, who will impart messages to me. When the chatter is gone and the mind quiets itself, it can be open to everything or even nothing at all. That's when you realize that silence can truly be golden.

3. *Be habitual*. Habits often get a negative rap because they are sometimes linked with the word *bad*. But developing good habits is beneficial to mental and physical health. I could go on here about developing good exercise and eating habits, but my real intent is to push good spiritual habits. Even if you claim membership to no church or are an atheist, spir-

itual habits like regular meditation put you in touch with your deeper self.

4. *Challenge anger.* In one landmark study, those who had experienced NDE were found to be type A with a lack of anger. That means they are among the most achievement driven of the population, yet don't experience anger nearly as often as the traditional achievement-oriented type A population. Why is that? Some researchers speculate that those who have had an NDE receive a blast of universal love during their experience, while others link a lack of anger with regular meditation practice.

This is good news, since research links lower anger and hostility with much lower death rates from heart disease and even addiction. This is why the emotional acceptance of the world is so important. A calm, easy, and accepting attitude toward life, an attitude granting that what will be will be, allows the world to show its infinite flavors as they are, not mixed with negative emotional baggage.

5. *Be optimistic.* Pessimism is low among those who have had an NDE, and it shows. They have better diets, drink less alcohol, have less work-related stress, and are less fearful of the future than the regular population. The reason for their optimism is a feeling that their lives are meaningful and their presence on this earth is important. Also they have a strong belief in an afterlife, which creates optimism because, well, *dead turned out not to be dead.* Negative emotions such as disappointment, fear, and anger tend to have caustic effects that contaminate life and sap it of its unique nature. By giving rise to a lot of chatter in our heads, nega-

tive emotion draws a veil over our perception of the world and tends to make everything hazy and indistinct and keeps us locked in our minds.

I realize these rules are simple, yet once we commit ourselves to them, they can have a profound effect on almost everything we do. They are the basis for our values, which determine whom we marry, the way we raise our children, how we treat our friends and neighbors, and a multitude of other crucial facets of our life. They remind me of something Mahatma Gandhi said to his followers: "Everything that you do in life is insignificant, yet it is important that you do it."

Chapter 21

An Experiment of One

It was a year and a half since my near-death experience, and I was physically whole. The infection in my abdomen had almost disappeared within a few days of surgery and never came back. The doctors were surprised at the rate at which the infection receded and allowed me to go home that week.

The antidepressants and pain pills I once took no longer interested me. But due to my medical codependence, I knew I had to cut back gradually, especially since my surgical wounds would take time to close.

The ultimate question for me was whether the NDE would really affect my recovery. Frankly I didn't know, or at least I didn't fully believe what I *did* know. I had been reading the medical literature on near-death experiences and found plenty of examples of physical and mental change taking place in NDEs.

Pim Van Lommel, in his classic book *Consciousness Beyond Life*, cites a number of physical changes as a result of NDEs, including sensitivity to sound, taste, touch, and smell; increased sensitivity to medications; and, most mysterious to me, "the ability to direct healing powers at others" and cases of "inexplicable self-healing after an NDE." One such case is cited in *Where God Lives*, by Melvin Morse, MD, and Paul Perry. In that case, a woman named Rita Klaus had a complete remission from multiple sclerosis, even in areas of her body thought to be permanently damaged.

On the day before her recovery, Klaus was at home waiting for her husband to finish watching the eleven o'clock news when she heard a "sweet" voice "inside me, outside me, all around me," say "Why don't you ask?"

She had prayed regularly but had not asked to be healed of her disease, she said. This time she felt "a sudden surge of electricity down the back of my neck and into my arms and legs . . . a sparkling feeling of bubbly champagne." She'd also had a near-death experience at the age of nine, which makes me think it was easier for her to have this spontaneous healing experience later in life.

Her physician, Dr. Donald Meister, is quoted as saying, "Spontaneous remissions of MS are possible. The only thing that doesn't fit in this case is that the permanent damage that occurs with MS does not go away (as it did for Rita). Whether or not this was divinely inspired is not for me to say. I'd love to know how it happened, and be able to use it again."

A case cited in another of Morse and Perry's books, *Transformed by the Light*, is a woman named Kathy who was diagnosed as having thyroid gland cancer. After radiation and chemotherapy, her doctor told her that the cancer had spread to other parts of her body and she probably had only six months to live.

As her cancer worsened, so did her immune system. Eventually she developed viral pneumonia and was readmitted to the hospital. There, her illness became worse and worse until one night her breathing and heart stopped. Doctors rushed into her room to start lifesaving procedures. Here's the story as Kathy tells it:

> Everything went very dark for a few seconds. Then suddenly I was way high on top of a ridge, overlooking a beautiful valley. The colors were extremely vivid, far more vivid than those I have previously experienced. It was marvelous. I was filled with a thrilling sense of joy.
>
> A Being was at my side, a Being of Light. Yet it wasn't like a Light that you see, but rather felt and understood. It touched me, and my whole body was filled with its Light. It was bursting out of me. I sensed a voice telling me that I could not enter the wonderful valley, that my children still needed me.

Almost miraculously, Kathy recovered from the pneumonia and the cardiac arrest. But a true miracle took place a few weeks later when Kathy's cancer disappeared.

Morse proposed a theory of healing with Kathy's case and others who had experienced a healing after a bright Light experience, whether during an NDE or a "spontaneous" experience of Light that can take place during transcendental experiences like periods of deep meditation. Morse believes that these "Light shouts" increase the body's electromagnetic force field, stimulating the pineal gland, a tiny nodule deep in the brain that secretes hormones that influence the working of the immune system. If this happens, the immune system could become far stronger and able to cure a variety of ailments, including cancer.

This Light shout also has effects on other important parts of the brain. It is Morse's belief that the right temporal lobe is affected. This area of the brain, known by some as the circuit board of mysticism, is the area responsible for complex language, self-consciousness, long-term planning, even daydreams. But it is also our link to the divine. The famed neurosurgeon Wilder Penfield called this area "the man within the man," or, as some might call it, "the soul."

This is the area in our brain that links to God or a transcendental plane. When it experiences a Light shout, as with an NDE or deep meditation in which Light appears, it can change us profoundly. Morse's groundbreaking transformation studies and the work of others has revealed that these Light shouts can change virtually everything in a person's life by affecting anxiety levels, confidence, diet, outlook on life, belief in God, death anxiety, and one's sense of the true meaning of life. In other words, everything that happened to me during my NDE!

Morse's work sounds theoretical. But some physicians use the principles of the Light shout to alter the body's electromagnetic field and heal difficult illnesses.

The late surgeon Margaret Patterson of Edinburgh, Scotland, developed neuroelectric therapy, a treatment that transformed substance abusers to nonaddictive personalities. Her treatment consisted of running weak electric current through the right temporal lobe. She had a very high success rate with this unusual and rarely practiced treatment, even with those addicted to heroin, a difficult addiction to break.

As a personal note, I feel as though I myself have been a beneficiary of the "Light shout" that took place during my NDE, and as a result, the clients I treat are beneficiaries as well. My experience with the Light has added a dimension of the supernatural to my own healing practice. And although I cannot yet fully define all of the elements of the consciousness-based healing that the angels told me to practice during my NDE, I can tell you that the Light has added elements of empathy and intuition that I did not have before my encounter, elements that I can use to become a better practitioner of the consciousness-based healing I was told to practice.

These elements come to me in the form of a universal energy received during the meditation I perform before treating a client. I know it sounds very "New Age" to speak of a universal energy, but that is the best description I can give to explain what happens. Sometimes this energy comes to me in the form of Light. Other times I am aware of the presence of my angelic friends. Every time I engage in these meditations, I am aware of the feeling of being "charged up" with a universal energy that provides me with the intuition that helps treat depression, addiction, and pain.

One such example of this healing comes from a woman I'll call Debbie. She lives in the Southeastern United States, in an area where, for lack of adequate laws, pain pills are readily available.

She had some minor pain in her back from sitting too much at her job and began taking pain pills, which soon turned into an addiction that led to a severe case of depression. As a result of this addiction she had lost focus in her personal and professional life and found herself drained of energy and emotion.

My first goal with Debbie when she contacted me was to talk with her about addiction, something no other professional had done. Then I got her on the path to consciousness-based healing by giving her the tools to consult her consciousness before following the path she had reflexively been following for so many years, the one that had her taking powerful pain killers all day long.

I taught her how to meditate and communicate with herself, gave her short meditation techniques and prayers to break those powerful urges that afflict addicts, and had her engage in acts of service to those less fortunate.

In a very short period of time her pill use tapered to almost nothing, and with it her depression diminished. The pain she had was nearly eliminated by the physical exercise I asked her to do, which led to weight loss that gave her a better body image.

Following these precepts of consciousness-based healing require self-effort, given that addictions always seem to reside just below the surface. But Debbie is now on the right path and says she plans to stay there. As she wrote to me: *I get up early in the morning now because I want to. I am filled with energy and gratitude, so much so that my family and friends are in awe. I am in awe too. I now have control of my life and intend to keep it that way.*

I bring up Debbie's case as an example of the ways in which I have been able to use the Light in my healing practice. *What has healed me can be passed on to you,* I tell my clients. *And you can also pass it on to those who need it. Example is the best teacher.*

———

"So what do you think all of this means?" asked Naresh.

We were having lunch together, and the conversation had turned to my studies in healing, which then led us to a frequent topic as of late: how to become one's own healer. The topic had become a favorite of mine because it's what consciousness-based healing is all about: reorienting the mind's focus from the physical to the spiritual. To find that mysterious connection to the spiritual world, we have to reach deep into ourselves. But where we reach is anyone's guess.

Many medical doctors and researchers think this connection is located in the right temporal lobe and go so far as to call this important area of the brain the "seat of the soul." Others are less specific, or sometimes even less physical. Rather than point to a specific region of the brain, they feel that one transcends the physical through the unconscious mind, defined by psychologist Carl Jung as "the collective unconscious," a reservoir of human experience from the beginning of humankind that resides in us all and binds us together in mystical ways. This includes, say some thinkers, our link with the divine. Still others feel that spirituality resides somewhere outside us.

In my estimation, nobody has the answer. It's almost like asking where heaven is, as in, *Is heaven in our mind or is it a place?* In fact, there is no correct answer, only opinion.

Where the spiritual resides is a question far too theoretical for most. But I do know that I found it during my NDE. As a result, I went to heaven, and I want to go back again without risking the death that is normally associated with the opportunity to enter heaven. *And* I know that the closest I have ever come to achieving that is with meditation. Through meditation, I have gone back to the Light several times, and it has healed me of addiction while helping me with depression and chronic pain in a way that powerful medications did not. That same Light has healed many others as well.

Speculation is rife as to where the healing Light comes from and exactly how it functions. My opinion is that it takes place when we somehow enter God's presence. Nonetheless, I don't need to know exactly how something works to use it effectively. I am an anesthesiologist by training, so I speak from experience and education when I say that no one really knows how anesthesia works. There is much speculation and many opinions, but the bottom line is that the mechanism behind anesthesia is a mystery even if its effects are not. This lack of specific knowledge doesn't keep us from using it. We dole out specific doses of anesthesia that kill pain so effectively that a patient sleeps through even the most invasive surgical procedures.

The same is true of near-death experiences and meditation. No one really knows how they heal or transform, but they do. Studies have shown that both NDEs and meditation have powerful healing properties.

How does this work? Once again the answer is not really known. Speculation abounds, and scientific studies are now being conducted to determine why NDEs and meditation heal. For now, I am trying to discover how to use these forces in physical and mental healing, in particular, for the benefit of my ill and very best friend, Naresh.

Naresh was interested in the possibility of spontaneous healing. I fully understood why. He was desperate now and very frightened. His cancer had metastasized and could no longer be kept in check by chemotherapy. He was losing weight, exhausted, and, most of all, frightened of leaving his family without him. He did not want to die, which is why he became interested in the Light shouts, those moments of spontaneous healing discussed by Melvin Morse and others.

"Sometimes they don't heal, but they make cancer treatable and contained," he said. "Why not me? Why wouldn't it work for me?"

Why not? I thought.

I knew in my own meditations, I could reach out and touch the spiritual world. But when the spiritual world reaches back, it gives me what I need, not necessarily what I want or even halfway expect. That's why meditation veterans say, "Let go, let God." It reminds them that we can only ask God for what we want and *hope* we get it. Insisting will get us nowhere.

"I know that already," said Naresh. "I know we can't control what we get from God. But at least I can try a meditation and see if it works."

So right then and there, in our favorite restaurant during lunch, I decided to design a meditation that I hoped would give him a Light shout. The basis for it was a meditation I learned at an ashram in the Himalayas. The guru who taught it to me called it the "inner Light" meditation because it was aimed at connecting to the spiritual Light that exists within us.

When I did it, I found it to be incredibly effective in seeing a spiritual Light. The Light itself was always different. Sometimes it came on slow and speckled, like starlight after sunset. Other times it came on strong and seemed to be accompanied by wind. Other times it was like a powerful flashbulb, a blast of Light that affected all of my senses with its power. I could never guess what the intensity of the Light would be or anticipate its effect. Sometimes it was very relaxing, and other times it left me feeling as though I had a charge of static electricity inside.

The guru told me to use this inner Light meditation to focus on issues one at a time. He said that the Light would change with the issue presented. Some issues demanded more of the Light than others. And, yes, though I would not always get what I want, maybe I would get what I need.

"Teach me that one," said Naresh.

I flipped the paper place mat over and wrote out the instructions for the meditation:

1. Sit cross-legged on the floor and relax so much that you can feel the weight of your body increase and the tension leave your body.
2. Clear your mind and become fully receptive to the world around you, letting thoughts pass through your mind without letting them stick.
3. Select one issue in your life; then focus on that issue. Step back from it and consider it from a distance, as though it is someone else's problem.
4. Close your eyes and ask what it is about this issue you would like to change.
5. While doing step 4, imagine total darkness and feel yourself completely absorbed in the issue you have come to examine. After several minutes, let the issue go.

6. Turn your attention to the deep darkness behind your eyelids. Let thoughts come and go without judgment or engagement for several minutes. If the Light comes, it will come now. Focus on it.

7. You may have revelations through the Light. Accept them even if they are emotionally painful. Acknowledge the feelings you receive from the Light.

"And finally, Naresh, if nothing happens don't be disappointed," I said, handing him the place mat. "Sometimes it takes several meditation sessions to see the Light, and sometimes it never happens."

That evening Naresh called with a progress report: "Nothing yet."

And so it went for several days as he diligently did his inner Light meditation with no success. Then one night it happened. As he reached the point where he went deep into the darkness, a bright Light emerged like a freight train. Naresh was alarmed for a moment, then settled down. He seemed surrounded by information of all kinds: his life whizzed past him in review, the universe seemed small and accessible, everything seemed to turn inside out in a way that he understood it, he felt a deep sense of love and understanding for all things. For a moment he saw a "beautiful place." Then he came back.

"Do you think you had a healing?" I asked.

"I don't know," he said. "But for a moment I had no fear or pain."

Naresh continued to practice the meditation almost daily and seemed joyful after having done it. Still, although it was a brief respite from his struggle against cancer, it did not give him the spontaneous remission he wanted. And despite finding some of the Light within, he continued to slip away down that long dark road.

Chapter 22

Aruba Awakening

By now, I had determined that meditation was the way to the soul, and the soul was the way to healing.

My reasoning was simple. Although our emotions come to life through our physical being, their roots lie in the soul. And although our emotions aren't a disease in and of themselves, they can lead to many diseases like high blood pressure, tachycardia, and clogged arteries and harmful reactions like grief, anger, lack of self-esteem, and depression. Emotions that are out of control often, if not always, have a link to the soul, the deepest and truest nature of our individual selves. The soul is the keeper of our private thoughts and the only entity that truly knows how we view ourselves.

I knew this firsthand before my NDE. Afterward I understood that my new mission was to heal myself and everyone else I could reach. The Being of Light called this "consciousness-based healing" and left me to create this holistic form of treatment, one firmly based in meditation.

I chose a visit to Aruba to hone my meditation skills. Not only is it a fabulous island in the Caribbean Sea, it was also where our son Raghav was going to medical school. I saw this as an opportunity to work on my relationship with my son as well as my relationship with myself through meditation.

I realize now I was living in ignorance regarding our son because I had placed my ego over his happiness. He attended school willingly, but didn't want to be there. Unfortunately I was ignoring that very obvious fact because I was choosing to live in the old ways.

In the culture of India, much is expected of the eldest son. It is his role to be the most driven of the children and the one who establishes the pattern of success for his siblings. Like many other immigrants (although my wife and I had lived in the United States for over twenty-five years and our children were all American born), we continued to live as if this Indian tradition was essential to our family's success.

But it wasn't bringing Raghav happiness. What he wanted was not what we wanted. And although he insisted he wanted to go to medical school when we questioned him, it was clear that his heart wasn't in it, that his desire to please us was causing him to silence his own dreams. He was fighting a battle between parental expectations and his own desires—his passion for computer science.

Meantime, I was fighting my own battle—one between my paternal expectations and my son's passion. I wanted my eldest son to follow in my footsteps, to become a medical doctor like the children of so many of our friends were doing. Only later would I realize that I had pushed him in that direction relentlessly, so relentlessly that he could not say no.

Instead of letting him lead his own life, I wondered what it was that he didn't understand. The better question would have been, What was it that I didn't understand? The answer was simple: I was stuck in an old paradigm, a myth, one that says "father knows best."

———

I worked on my meditation skills not only to get better in my own practice but to develop different meditations that could be used by those in need of consciousness-based healing. There are many states that can be achieved by meditation, and I felt that I could achieve them all. Practice makes perfect, and when it came to meditation, I had already been engaged in deep and daily practice and expected greater results on this island paradise.

I was surprised to suddenly find myself a victim of meditation block. Meditation block is like writer's block, only instead of not being able to write, I found myself unable to meditate. It began in earnest after my first week on the island. I took a long morning walk down a white sand beach, staying close to the leading edge of the waves that reached out from the bright blue ocean.

After a couple of miles of walking, I sat cross-legged in the soft sand and faced the sun, closing my eyes to practice a gratitude meditation, one that had me thanking my higher power for the gift of another sunrise.

My meditation went nowhere. Instead of slipping into the state of intense comfort where I felt grateful for all of the good that surrounded me, I felt, oddly enough, intense unhappiness at having to be here in Aruba instead of home in California. Everything negative in my life lined up in front of me and would not pass. Thoughts like this can arise during ordinary meditation, but I had learned to accept them and let them pass harmlessly by to wherever negative thoughts go. But now on Aruba, the negative thoughts would not pass. Instead they stopped and taunted me like the monsters of the mind they were. Soon my relaxing meditations turned into negative and disordered episodes.

I tried a variety of techniques to turn my meditations around. I tried mindfulness meditation where I focused on my belly and concentrated on bringing my breath in and out of that spot. That couldn't get me past my negative thoughts. Body scan meditation, in which I focused on a different part of the body with each breath, didn't take my mind off the monsters that taunted me. I did walking meditation, slowly pacing back and forth on a patch of warm sand, the goal being to focus on each step, trying to feel the bottom of each foot while looking at a neutral spot in the distance. This time there was no neutral spot, just painful visions and memories. No matter what I did, I could not get the monsters to leave me alone. When I closed my eyes to enter the cool and calm heaven of meditation, I found myself in the disorderly hell of anger and resentment. This went on for weeks and led me to lose confidence and fear that the spiritual effects of my NDE had left me for good. No matter how I tried, I could not get spiritual traction.

Unfairly, I blamed this failure of meditation on my father or paths not taken in my life. But when I tried to push these thoughts out of my head, I could feel a pulse of anger and resentment every time. At times I even unfairly blamed this failure of meditation on Raghav, which made for some icy evenings. I had counted on my meditation to keep me focused and calm; without it, I could feel the pulse of anger and resentment every time I suggested Raghav study more or (heaven forbid) that he let me help him study.

I could tell that the resentment went both ways. "I wish you hadn't come," he said to me one day.

"I wish the same," I said.

Looking back, I can see that I was not acting with empathy or compassion but out of ego. I wanted what I wanted—a son to become a medical doctor—and I didn't care how he felt. Yes, *father knows best.*

Then one day I had a breakthrough. On a stretch of beach, I stopped and faced the sun. Anger was welling inside where I should have had peace. My mind was scattered when it should have been living firmly in the now. I prayed a single sentence: *What do I do next?*

Words from the angels came into my head loud and clear: *Show compassion.*

I nearly choked up with shame. *I'm not showing compassion,* I said to myself. My assignment from the Being of Light was to create a field of medicine based largely on compassion, yet I had let my dark side take over, the side of my ego that made me think only about me. I needed to forgive, love, and heal. I needed to drop the notion that father knows best. The fact was that I didn't know what was best for Raghav. He was doing what I wanted, but the payoff for him was unhappiness. After all, every day in school put him closer to becoming a doctor, a life that would make him miserable. I was wrong to push him without asking him where he wanted to go.

Father does not know best, I told myself.

It was a harsh realization for me, but within a moment I knew I had arrived. I felt as though I had stepped through a wall and into a new world of freedom and understanding. It had been the purpose of the meditation block, which I now saw as being a blessing and not a curse. I was free of my ego.

I sat down under a tree and took out a pad and pen. Then for the next hour, I wrote down instructions for the following meditation:

FORGIVENESS MEDITATION

Healing is directly linked to forgiveness. Release from any dis-ease—physical, mental, or emotional—can only happen when there is internal ease, and that requires the capacity to forgive.

Forgiving isn't the same as forgetting. We don't want to pretend that the things that once hurt us never happened. We want to be able to recall them without them causing us any more hurt. It also won't mean that we rush to socialize or reengage with those whom we are forgiving. We can forgive effectively within our heart without ever needing to meet someone again to make the healing complete. The purpose of the forgiveness is to release ourselves from the past, not to renew or remake our chains to it.

Time: One hour

THINGS TO DO

Switch your phone off and play music or surround yourself with peaceful sounds of nature. Sitting comfortably, close your eyes. Breathe in and out, relaxing more and more with every exhalation. As you breathe in, visualize your spinal column being filled with white Light. As you breathe out, visualize the Light spreading from your spine across your body. Continue to breathe in and out until the Light has spread from your spine across your whole body. Every cell of your body is now infused with glowing white Light.

Now as you see yourself with a body of pure white Light, imagine that you are standing in a garden of flowers with a healing lake in its center. Imagine that you look into the lake and see yourself. Your reflection is of you as a child, when you were maybe four or five or six years old. The child needs you to take care of them. Tell the child you love them, and that they are safe. Tell the child that you will always love them and always forgive them no matter what mistakes they make. Hold the child tight, showering all your love on them, letting them know you will never abandon them and that you will always protect them. Tell the child they deserve love and success and peace in life. Tell the child you will always help them find their way again if they ever get lost, no matter how big their mistakes. See the child smiling, playing contentedly knowing you are there for them. Tell the child whenever they need you, you will always respond.

Look up from the lake and feel the white Light from your body emanate throughout the flower garden. Feel the sweetness of the flowers come into your Light.

Now look in the lake again. This time imagine that you see the face of your parents as they were as little children. Imagine that they ask you to forgive them for everything they have ever done to you that may have caused you sorrow. Look at them with love as children and let them know that you will no longer be angry with them. You forgive them and love them and they should no longer worry. See them smiling happily, showering affection and love on you as they play.

Look up from the lake and feel the white Light from your body emanate throughout the flower garden. Breathe the sweetness of the flowers into your Light body.

Keep returning to the lake as many times as you feel you want to, seeing all the people who have ever touched your life: your siblings, parents, colleagues, spouse, children.

See them each as little children looking out at you with the innocence and concern of children who have done something they did not mean to do. As they each tell you they're sorry and ask for your forgiveness, feel yourself loving them as children and let them know they are safe, and everything is okay, and that they can be at peace and play. As you tell them everything is okay, feel them showering you with love and see them smiling with the sweetness and innocence of children.

When every last person has gone from the lake, look back in the lake. See yourself as an adult. See yourself looking peaceful, and radiant, and happy. You feel safe and secure and loved and loving. You are overcome with joy. All the cells of your body are vibrating in perfect health. You hear yourself saying, "Thank you for being here for me. I love you." Imagine that your white Light body and the reflection in the lake and the sweetness of the flowers all merge together.

Breathe in: "All is forgiven in my world" and breathe out: "All is well"—until you feel you are ready to open your eyes.

Lastly, in your journal, write down any conversations or messages you had with anyone who came to the lake. Record how you feel.

I performed that meditation successfully, imagining my childhood in a better light. As I did so, my love for my father was rekindled. Thoughts and feelings about my father drifted into thoughts and feelings I had about my own parenting. The most profound of all were these questions: *Have you been practicing a form of materialism by pushing Raghav to become a doctor? And is pride a form of materialism?*

I needed to answer those questions.

Chapter 23

Be Who You Are

When Raghav was in class, I spent my time developing meditations, spending hours reading works of religious and spiritual importance for the common threads that bind all forms of spiritual thought. I also deconstructed my NDE to consider the types of meditation that would work best to reach each of the levels of consciousness I had experienced.

In the evening I visited Raghav until he dismissed me to continue his studies. He was in the groove now, studying until midnight and getting up early to make it to class. I was thrilled. *Maybe Raghav does want to be a medical doctor,* I thought, trying to keep my ego under wraps. *He sure is studying like one.*

My forgiveness meditations had opened me to be more compassionate in general, especially to my son. In the course of developing empathy, I began to realize how hard I had pushed him to complete medical school. With that realization came the question that had arisen during so many of my meditations: *Has your pride been trying to force him to be something he does not want to be?*

Father knows best, I thought. But only as it relates to father.

And then before we knew it, the semester was over and Raghav had passed his final exams. He was now in his third year of medical school. One more year and he would have his medical degree.

We returned to California in time for Thanksgiving. Arpana met us at the airport, and all of us were beaming with joy. Then suddenly Raghav hugged me around the neck, and I cried. Arpana reached over and wiped tears from my cheeks.

"Thanks for your help, Dad," he said. "Thanks to both of you."

My thoughts went back to my NDE and all of the days in between. It had been a long road, but I was thrilled for all that had happened and the spiritual breakthroughs in my life. I had learned a lot. Now I was about to learn more.

———————

Before the next semester began, Raghav had to pass the US Medical Licensing Examination (USMLE), a medical proficiency exam to see how well he understood basic medical sciences and apply them to the practice of medicine. It's a difficult exam, but one that medical schools insist students pass to make certain they have the aptitude to continue with their schooling.

I felt as though Raghav was fully prepared to study for the test. We discussed what it would take to pass the exam and create an environment in the house where he could study. Then Arpana and I left him alone to do the work. By giving him free rein, we could see if he truly wanted to become a doctor or wanted to strike out on a different path.

During this period, my ego slipped back into view. I began to think that my success would be enhanced if my son became a medical doctor. But what if he didn't want to be a doctor? What if he didn't succeed with the exam? Would my father's wrath manifest itself in me again, as it had before my NDE? Would I become demanding and angry if he did not choose to become a medical doctor? To stave off my fears, I chose the counsel of Naresh, still struggling valiantly against cancer.

He listened to my lament and then offered his opinion. "What really matters is that your son enjoys his life," he said. "I know that truth now because I'm sick. You know it because of your NDE. Your son knows it in his own way. I don't think he really wants to be a medical doctor but he's afraid to tell you. Ask him what he wants to do with his life; don't tell him. Remember, it's his life."

I called my sister in India and told her what was going on. She had lost her son two years before. He had graduated from business school in Singapore on a Friday and on Sunday night was killed in an automobile accident. She listened patiently and then offered her opinion.

"Be glad that you have him," she said. "I would do anything to have that problem."

Finally I asked Arpana. "Just love him for what he is," she said. "That is one of the messages you received during your NDE, isn't it? *Change by example, not by force.* We just have to face the fact that he doesn't want to become a doctor."

And so I quit asking my friends and family what they thought of this dilemma. Instead I asked Raghav.

Arpana and I were standing in the kitchen. Raghav was passing through the family room when I asked him to stop for a minute.

Arpana knew something was coming. She was drinking a glass of water but set the glass down and pulled Raghav close to her. It was a protective move, one that made me feel shame in knowing they feared an abusive outcome.

"How are your studies going?" I asked.

"Not good," said Raghav. "I can't stay interested."

"Do you want to become a doctor?" I asked.

"I've tried," he said. "I don't want to disappoint you two. I don't know what to say, but it's not for me."

I looked at Raghav. We looked at each other. I could feel his discomfort, and this time it filled me with compassion instead of anger. *How difficult it must be for him to talk about this. How fearful he must feel,* I thought.

All I could think about was how to make it easier on him. *What can I do that will lighten his load and restore his hopes for the future? What role can I play in supporting him to navigate the path ahead?* For once I was far more concerned about his needs than my own. Now it was inconceivable for me to reproach him, chastise him, or shame him as I feared I might. If anything, I was filled with sorrow at the way I had handled such moments in the past.

As the three of us stood together in the kitchen, I felt an unstoppable commitment to being his father, a desire to guide, support, and coach him toward independence and success. I knew that I needed to start doing this in ways that would allow him to affirm his natural talent and skills and not be forced to adapt to mine.

I cleared my throat.

"We'll move on then," I said. "You're young. It's best this happens before you're older and can't make a change."

I watched as my beloved wife and son exhaled. I told him I would help him, no matter what was required of me. The lesson was clear to me: Life's biggest problems can come from trying to live up to someone else's expectations and forgetting your own.

The path with my son was now to help him figure out who he was and to nurture his passions, not tell him what they were. *Why am I on earth if not to ease the suffering of someone I care for?* I thought.

And with that realization, my relationship with my son changed completely.

Chapter 24

A Shared-Death Experience

All these months Naresh had continued to meditate, even when I was in Aruba with my son. But despite his efforts, he never got that healing Light shout he had hoped for. In the end, he accepted his fate.

I was often with him during the last few days of his life, watching hopelessly as he slipped away. His wife, Neelam, was there, holding his hand and talking to him as he tried weakly to keep the conversation going. When she wasn't there, I held his hand, and we tried to ignore the presence of death in the room. There was very little we could say about the future, knowing that he had just a few tomorrows left. But we talked about things from our past, and he compiled a sort of bucket list of things he wished he had done in his short life. The one that brought a lump to both of our throats was when he said he would like to see his children grow up.

The subject of meditation and yoga came up, and he was glad to have practiced both because they reduced his level of physical and mental pain. This was especially true of the Light shout meditation, he insisted. Even though it did not give him the spontaneous healing he had hoped for, it did provide peace.

"I'm sorry it didn't work," I told him.

"It did," he said. "I experienced a very bright Light many times, which I didn't expect. But better than that, it put me at peace. That is success too."

On his last day, I visited. He could feel my touch, but he was in a coma from which he would not return.

I went home and spoke to Arpana for a while. Even though I know what happens when we die, it was still sad for me to see a friend go. I was going to miss Naresh terribly, I told Arpana. He was a good friend. Arpana's sad eyes told me she felt the same.

That night as I slept, a bright Light awoke me. Incredibly, I saw and felt Naresh. He was in his spiritual body appearing much younger and smiling. My room was lit up by his presence, and I found myself floating outside my body. The room's dimension began to freakishly expand, moving as if magically ballooning into a spherical-oblique space. The room felt multidimensional and to this day is hard for me to describe.

I stood holding hands with Naresh, saying nothing, when a portal opened above us and flooded the room with more Light. Together we floated into the portal, climbing steadily toward a bright Light that beamed like a thousand suns yet did not hurt my eyes.

I felt the presence of the Being of Light, the same Being I had encountered during my NDE. This time, however, a Being emerged from the Light, a tall man with a pale-brown complexion and a beard, wearing a majestic white gown. Most memorable were his deep blue eyes. He was radiating unconditional love.

"Who are you?" I asked the Being.

"I am Jesus, your savior," he responded.

I bowed immediately and in Indian custom said "Namaste" while touching his feet. He placed his hand over my head and blessed me. He told me it was not my time to leave earth and that I had to go back and spread his message of universal love, of Christ consciousness.

We hugged, and he said something that gave me direction: "From now on your spiritual name will be Michael. You are to be strong and brave and help the sick."

With a great suddenness, the ground parted, leaving a deep canyon between us. On one side I stood, and on the other side were Jesus, Naresh, and other Beings of Light.

Then I awoke.

I found myself sitting up in bed, staring at the place where the portal had been. I didn't immediately know what this meant to me personally, but I did know that Naresh was close to passing from this earth if he hadn't done so already.

I awoke Arpana and told her what had just happened.

"You need to call Neelam immediately," she said.

In the early-morning hours, I grappled for the phone but decided not to make the call. I didn't want to disturb Neelam at the end of her husband's life. I decided instead to lie back down and give him my prayers.

Later that morning when I arrived at Naresh's home, his wife told me the hour he had died. It was at the same time the portal opened in my room and the Light of heaven shone in.

Conclusion

To Understand
Who We Are

*The artist is no other than he who unlearns what he has
learned, in order to know himself.*

e. e. cummings

With the shared-death experience I'd had with Naresh, I knew I
was suddenly on another path and that my dharma had changed.
But where was it taking me? I'd had a shared-death experience in
which a healthy individual accompanies a dying loved one on his
or her final journey. These experiences have been recorded since
primitive times. But now mine had a twist: I had been blessed to
be in the presence of Jesus.

I didn't know what that meant and didn't quite know what to
do. At first consideration, I thought I was being asked to convert
to Christianity, but as I thought further, I realized it might be
something different altogether. Jesus had asked me to "spread [the]

message of universal love, of Christ consciousness," not necessarily convert to Christianity. He told me that from now on, my name would be Michael, which I assumed put me in a role similar to that of the archangel Michael. Once again that seemed like a call to convert. But then I remembered Saint Michael's history and how he was considered the archangel of God by Christians, Catholics, Eastern Orthodox religions, and even some Jews.

As a Hindu called on to change his name to Michael and spread the message of Christ consciousness, wouldn't I reach more people by sending all religions one message: "forgive, love, heal"?

For some time I had planned to visit my mother in India. As always, I looked forward to seeing her and being in the grace of her presence. But on the long flight to New Delhi, I couldn't get thoughts of the encounter with Jesus out of my mind. After several restless days in New Delhi, I decided to take a few days off from my home visit to settle the questions within my mind. I chose to do that at a Buddhist meditation camp high in the Himalayas, one that could be reached most effectively by a train known as the Jammu Tawi Express.

My guilt at temporarily leaving my mother dissipated when the train left New Delhi for the city of Pathankot, a ride that took me through other Indian cities as well as miles of open countryside. In Pathankot, I left the train and jumped in a taxi for the most mountainous part of the journey. The taxi wound its way up the mountains and through the Himalayan valleys. The dense cities of India melted away, replaced by steep mountains, deep valleys, and dark green forests. The taxi driver drove so close to the edge that I felt as if we were hanging in thin air over a sheer cliff.

Hairpin turns and narrow roads bordered by high cliffs and steep valleys brought my heart to my mouth. There were no traffic rules to be followed, only the judgment and daring of the drivers themselves. It took me some time to get over the vertigo caused by the sway of the taxi and the sense of imminent disaster, but once I did, the beauty around me was heaven on earth.

At Dharamshala, the home of the exiled Dalai Lama, I left the taxi and was thankful to put my feet on solid ground.

The cab ride had rattled me, and when I began to talk about it at the meditation camp, I was shushed by a monk and told to be silent unless the guru spoke to me. Then he gave me my first assignment: meditate at least eight hours per day.

Such focus on clearing the mind is often accomplished by repeating a word, or mantra. In this camp, however, the focus was to be on breathing rather than a mantra, a type of meditation called Vipassana. We students were instructed to focus on our breath as we breathed in and breathed out. By doing this we would clear our minds so they could be (we hope) refilled with revelation.

The battle within my mind had intensified during the train trip to the camp. *Should I add Christianity and all the other major religions to my religious beliefs? Is that even possible?* These questions occupied my mind for the first two days of meditation, replacing my focus on breathing and making me fitful.

Then I had a breakthrough. It was the seventh day of these lengthy meditations. I was in my sixth hour when suddenly my body started shaking and my breathing became fast and chaotic. I felt warm, and a tingling sensation left me perspiring. An energy wave swept from the bottom of my spine up to my head. I could hear a "pop" signifying the opening of my chakras, those nodes of energy that line the body and affect its subtle energy field.

When the energy wave reached the crown chakra at the top of my head, my breathing became slow and deep, and in place of anxiety I felt supreme bliss and unconditional love. This state of awareness, called a Kundalini awakening, is an experience of deep meditation that can lead to the deepest of meditative states. And so it was for me.

I passed through a field of white light that left me feeling a deep love for all people I knew. Then the light faded, and I went into a deep darkness, one so dark it was palpable. To me it felt like a black hole, a void of emptiness and nothingness. I felt my selfness peel away until there was no individuality left. I was truly one with the universe.

I told my meditation teacher what had happened, and when I described it as a spiritual black hole, he laughed and said I had experienced "zeroness," which he defined as "the realm where there is no realm, the cosmic void, the nothingness."

"Congratulations," he said with that giggle of good humor so common among Buddhist holy men. "You have reached cosmic bliss."

The days following this experience were truly ones of bliss. I lost all personal desire. I had no wants, no needs, and no ego. I became one with what the meditation instructor called the "Greater." I accepted my life for what it was and wanted nothing but to live it with humble acceptance as it unfolded.

In this state I devised a new mantra: *Whatever is happening is perfect, and that's the way it is and should be.*

After visiting the spiritual black hole, I made a decision to serve all religions, from Christian to Hindu and all others. I felt there was a consciousness common to them all, one that I have come to call "universal consciousness."

I realized immediately that even in my own family, there was a way to use this new consciousness. My daughter had been dating a Muslim for several years. Being raised with my father's deep hatred of Muslims, I had had great difficulty in accepting her choice of a boyfriend. But now I understood the Muslim faith and the goodness that can come from this religion's consciousness. I was able to accept my daughter's friend and accept him in our lives. I have learned that *knowledge enlightens and heals.*

The source of my personal enlightenment has been my NDE. I think about it daily and am grateful for the life lessons it has taught me. From my brush with death and my NDE:

- *I have learned* my true religion. It is very simple. My religion is kindness and love. It welcomes all religions by looking for the sameness in them, not the differences.

- *I have discovered* my true calling: to endow others with a knowledge that encourages the body, mind, and spirit's natural ability to heal addiction and depression without following a pill-based approach.

- *I have learned* that materialism is an addiction that takes our focus away from selfless service to others, *seva,* the most rewarding thing we can do for ourselves. *Seva* is not just any kind of service, but service performed with a sense of gratitude. In India it is called "work offered to God" and is directed toward the poor, aged, or ill. It is service infused with kindness and respect for the ones served, and it gives rise to peace and love. It is an act of mental and emotional adjustment in a direction away from ourselves and toward the needs of others and of humanity as a whole.

• *I have learned* that if we nurture our relationships in accordance with *seva*, the world will change profoundly. *Seva* is not about taking a few hours out of our busy week to help others. *Seva* is about designing our lives in such a way that we consistently serve others selflessly, especially those less fortunate than us. As a Taoist verse says, "I work at eliminating all my judgment of others."

• *I have learned* that we can even take *seva* into the bedroom with us. With *seva* you do not simply aim for your own personal satisfaction. Instead, you focus on pleasing your partner, giving all you can to make her or him happy. As *The Wisdom of the Tao* tells us, "It is through selfless action that I experience my own fulfillment."

• *I have learned* to base my fatherhood on love, not anger.

• *I have created* my own Near-Death Manifesto: seven basic truths that provide guidance and comfort on a daily basis:
    1. Consciousness can exist outside the body.
    2. There is life after death.
    3. We have past lives, and our experiences therein can shape our current realities.
    4. We are all connected to each other because we are all made of the one and same energy that manifests as differentiated matter.
    5. Divine beings exist to help and guide us.
    6. There are different levels of consciousness.
    7. There is one, all-pervading, supreme love and intelligence that is the source of the entire universe, and that love is the supreme source of creation.

- *I have learned* to love passionately, forgive easily, and heal quickly.

- *I have learned* to be happy.

- *I have learned* that the paranormal is, perhaps, the new normal.

- *And through my NDE* I have learned the true purpose of our lives: to understand who we are.

ACKNOWLEDGMENTS

There are many people to thank on the road to telling this story. My late father, Jagdish Chander Parti, is the first who comes to mind. Although he was a demanding father, sometimes to the point of harshness, he taught me many life lessons that are with me until this day. "If you keep your conscience clear and be truthful to yourself, the universe and the divine will take care of you" were the last words he spoke to me before he died and among the first he reminded me of when we met again on the other side. I both feared and missed him when he died, but after he rescued me from the rim of hell I understood him and felt great empathy for the difficulty he had experienced in his life. One of his most precious goals was to make sure that I could be all that I could be. I thank him for that and now truly miss him. Our relationship forms the backbone of this book and his words the framework for my new life.

My nephew, Siddharth Kamal, also plays an important role in my story. The son of my youngest sister, Siddharth's life tragically ended in 2011 at the age of twenty-one in a car accident. Only two days before, this joyful, handsome and loving young man had graduated from Singapore Management University with so many dreams about his life ahead. As curious about the history of Scotch as he was about saints, Siddharth lived up to his name—"the prince who always shined." He believed and often said, "You only live once but if you live right, once is enough." As you know I believe he is wrong about living only once, and look forward to proving him wrong. Until then, Namaste, Siddharth, and much love to your mother and father, Monica and Sanjeev.

The women in my life have been a tremendous help. My wife, Arpana, encouraged and supported me through my cancer surgeries, bouts of depression, and subsequent transformation resulting from my NDE. For that I have great thanks. My mother, Swaran Parti, has been the greatest influence in my life. She comforted me during my difficult childhood, keeping me calm, focused, and on the path to success. It is her love, wisdom, and encouragement that I carry with me on a daily basis and that has sustained me in writing this book. My sisters, Minu and Monica, are my best friends. From childhood to the present day, their loyalty and solace has no equal. Along with my daughter, Ambika, these women are living angels in my life.

My sons, Raghav and Arjun, have been quietly supportive of the transformations my NDE have brought to the family. I especially thank Raghav for allowing me to present his story. He is now happily studying computers, the profession of his choice.

My late friend Naresh Dave, gave me the greatest gift of all, his undivided attention, as I struggled with personal and spiritual issues after having my NDE. I am thankful for his friendship.

Most everyone has unofficial coaches in their lives, people who guide us toward a desired goal. Two years before this book came out, my coauthor introduced me to two people who have been guiding lights for me. The first was Raymond Moody, MD, the physician who defined and named the near-death experience. The second was his literary agent, Nat Sobel. Both of those gentlemen have helped guide me as I told my story through Paul Perry. The three of them—Raymond, Nat, and Paul—are the reason this book is now in your hands. In this regard I also owe a debt of gratitude to Denise Gibbon, whose legal skills might well be exceeded by her substantial understanding of human psychology. This book has reached you through Johanna Castillo, vice president and executive editor at Atria Books/Simon and Schuster, who saw in it a message of forgiveness, love, and healing so needed in the twenty-first century.

I have two *official* coaches who have helped me overcome obstacles that would ordinarily have kept me from my first attempts to tell this story. Jo McGinley, a speech coach and actress, has helped me overcome my fear of public speaking. Creativity coach Srikumar Rao, PhD, of the Rao Institute, taught me how to incorporate spirituality and inspiration into every corner of my life, adding more meaning to each and every day.

Jill Mangino has done excellent work in bringing this book to public attention through her public relations agency, Circle 3 Media. Raquel Sofer helped me early on to organize my thoughts about my NDE and the science surrounding it. Thanks also goes to Alana Karran who taught me how to organize many of my early talks.

One of the true blessings has been in meeting people who have also had NDEs. Among those who stand out are Dannion Brinkley, whose book *Saved by the Light* is a classic in NDE literature, Eben Alexander, MD, the Harvard-trained surgeon who wrote *Proof of Heaven*, and Anita Moorjani, whose cancer was miraculously cured by an NDE when she was at the very brink of death. Anita is an amazing individual whose mysterious recovery is explored in her book *Dying to Be Me*. Anita and her story have inspired me to listen and learn from my NDE.

Following the personal advice of Deepak Chopra, MD—"if you truly want to learn about spirituality, then speak in public about your NDE"—I spoke at several organizations interested in transcendent experiences. David Sunfellow, director of the Near-Death Experience Network in Sedona, gave me my first opportunity to speak about my NDE. After the warm reception given me by Sunfellow and his organization, I made the rounds of several chapters of the International Association of Near Death Experiences (IANDS). To each of the local chapter leaders I offer individual appreciation, including: Beverly Brodsky (San Diego), Denis Purcell (Los Angeles), Chuck Swedrock and Susan Amsden (Tucson, Arizona), Robin Barr and Bob Siress (Orange County, California), John Sphar (Southbay near San Francisco), Ellie Schamber (Marin County), Larry Merril (Mesa, Arizona), David Bourdon (Berkeley), Barbara Bartolome (Santa Barbara), and Diane Willis (Chicago). Special thanks goes to Diane Corcoran, president of IANDS, who graciously allowed me to speak and teach at the 2014 national conference. Also I wish to thank Karen Koebnick of Stellar Productions in Sedona, who brought me twice to the red rock country of Sedona, Arizona, to speak at her conferences.

The belief that consciousness survives bodily death is the backbone of near-death studies. Eternea is one such organization devoted to this field of study. Co-founded by Eben Alexander, MD, and John Audette, MS, Eternea explores near-death experiences and other spiritually transformative events in a way that is entertaining and educational. Visit their website at: http://eternea.org/.

For those who would like to contact me to tell of their own NDE, please go to: www.dyingtowakeup.com so we can carry on a dialogue beyond this book. It is by sharing the blessing in our lives that we develop a greater appreciation for one another and the world we live in.

Rajiv Parti, MD